1 CORINTHIANS

1 CORINTHIANS

JEROME MURPHY-O'CONNOR

DOUBLEDAY BIBLE COMMENTARY
DOUBLEDAY
NEW YORK • LONDON • TORONTO • SYDNEY • AUCKLAND

DOUBLEDAY BIBLE COMMENTARY
PUBLISHED BY DOUBLEDAY
a division of Bantam Doubleday Dell Publishing Group, Inc.
1540 Broadway, New York, New York 10036

DBC, DOUBLEDAY, and the portrayal of an anchor with a dolphin are trademarks of
Doubleday, a division of Bantam Doubleday Dell Publishing Group, Inc.

Library of Congress Cataloging-in-Publication Data

Murphy-O'Connor, J. (Jerome), 1935–
1 Corinthians / Jerome Murphy-O'Connor. — 1st U.S. ed.
p.   cm. — (Doubleday Bible commentary)
1. Bible. N.T. Corinthians, 1st—Commentaries. I. Title
II. Series
BS2675.3.M87   1998
227′.207—dc21   98-15196
CIP

ISBN 0-385-49022-4

DOUBLEDAY
BIBLE COMMENTARY
SERIES

Congratulations! You are embarking on a voyage of discovery—or redis-covery. You may feel you know the Bible very well; you may never have turned its pages before. You may be looking for a fresh way of approaching daily Bible study; you may be searching for useful insights to share in a study group or from a pulpit.

The Doubleday Bible Commentary (DBC) series is designed for all those who want to study the scriptures in a way that will warm the heart as well as instruct the mind. To help you, the series distills the best of scholarly insights into the straightforward language and devotional empha-sis of a daily Bible guide. Explanations of background material, and dis-cussions of the original Greek and Hebrew, will always aim to be brief.

• If you have never really studied the Bible before, the series offers a serious yet accessible way in.

• If you help to lead a church study group, or are otherwise involved in regular preaching and teaching, you can find invaluable "snapshots" of a Bible passage through the DBC approach.

• If you are a church worker or minister, burned out on the Bible, this series could help you recover the wonder of scripture.

USING A DOUBLEDAY
BIBLE COMMENTARY

THE SERIES IS designed for use alongside any version of the Bible. You may have your own favorite translation, but you might like to consider using a different one in order to gain fresh perspectives on familiar passages.

Many Bible translations come in a range of editions, including study and reference editions that have concordances, various special kinds of special indexes, maps, and marginal notes. These can all prove helpful in studying the relevant passage. The Notes section at the back of each DBC volume provides space for you to write personal reflections, points to follow up, questions, and comments.

Each Doubleday Bible Commentary can be used on a daily basis. Alternatively, it can be read straight through, or used as a resource book for insight into particular verses of the biblical book.

If you have enjoyed using this commentary and would like to progress further in Bible study, you will find details of other volumes in the series listed at the back.

While it is important to deepen understanding of a given passage, this series always aims to engage both heart and mind in the study of the Bible. The scriptures point to our Lord himself and our task is to use them to build our relationship with him. When we read, let us do so prayerfully, slowly, reverently, expecting him to speak to our hearts.

Contents

INTRODUCTION

PAUL HAD LIVED in busy cities. Tarsus, Jerusalem, Damascus, Antioch, and Athens were important centers with cosmopolitan populations. Yet when Paul came to Schoenus, rather wearily after his long two-day walk from Athens, he must have rubbed his eyes in amazement. Schoenus was the eastern terminus of the paved road linking the Saronic Gulf and the Corinthian Gulf at the narrowest point of the isthmus by which the Peloponnese hung like a leaf from mainland Greece.

This road was the crucial transfer point for east-west trade that preferred to avoid the risk of sailing around Cape Malea, the southern tip of the Peloponnese. Ant-like lines of laborers moved backward and forward continuously. They hauled small ships on a special carriage whose wheels ran in grooves in the pavement. The cargoes of larger ships had to be unloaded and moved piecemeal to the other terminal. The crackling energy of the scene, the bustle and the noise were like nothing that Paul had ever experienced before. It had the impact of a blow. This was the dynamism that had won for Corinth the qualification "wealthy" since the time of Homer. Paul would be forgiven for wondering if people so busy would ever have time to listen to the gospel.

The Choice of Corinth

AFTER BEING FORCED out of Beroea, Paul fled south to Athens (Acts 17:10–15). The once-glorious cultural center of Greece had fallen on evil days. It was an old, sick city without vitality, turned in on itself. Tradition was venerated in order to hold the threat of novelty at bay. Very quickly Paul realized that his preaching would be just another philosophy to be debated.

Corinth, on the other side of the Saronic Gulf, was a very different city. Its location on the isthmus made it the crossroads of north-south as well as east-west trade. For this reason it was refounded by Julius Caesar in 44 B.C., and quickly became the leading trading center in the eastern Mediterranean. Within two generations it was producing millionaires. It was a city of the self-made, and lived for the future. Its people were skeptical and preoccupied, but new ideas were guaranteed a hearing because profit was to be found in the strangest places.

Paul could see several advantages in preaching at Corinth. He would at least be assured a hearing, and to succeed in establishing a church in such a materialistic environment would be indisputable evidence of the power of the gospel. All the world knew the proverb: "Not for everyone is the voyage to Corinth." It was no place for the timid or the gullible. To convert hard-headed Corinthians would be a triumph of grace. Finally, the situation of Corinth guaranteed Paul superb communications. He could be virtually certain of finding someone to carry a letter anywhere.

The Foundation of the Church

ACCOMPANIED BY SILVANUS and Timothy (2 Corinthians 1:19), Paul arrived in Corinth sometime in the late spring or early summer of A.D. 50. He found work and lodging with Prisca and Aquila, Christians who had been expelled from Rome by the emperor Claudius in A.D. 41 (Acts 18:1–3), and with whom he shared the trade of tentmaker. While with them he wrote two letters to the Thessalonians.

Even though he operated from a small workshop, which identified him as a despised manual laborer, Paul's first converts were decidedly upper-class (1 Corinthians 1:14–16). They had the leisure to assist his efforts, and owned the sort of house in which the community could assemble (Romans 16:23). He must have targeted them as a matter of policy. His success reveals the power of his personality.

For different reasons the names of members of the community are mentioned in Acts 18:1–18; 1 Corinthians 1:14–16; 16:15–17; and Romans 16:21–24. They are not complete or systematic lists. They imply a minimum of between forty and fifty Christians at Corinth. The vast majority were of pagan origin, but had some association with the Jewish synagogue.

A number suffered from "status inconsistency." Their stature in their own eyes was not accepted by society at large. Prisca and Aquila, for example, were successful businesspeople, but they were Jews, outsiders who resided in the city on sufferance. Erastus (Romans 16:23) had achieved the second most important post in the administration of Corinth but believed that everyone saw him only as the son of a slave. They were attracted to the gospel because it embodied the paradox they lived. The idea of a savior who had died under torture spoke to the contradictions of their existence. Power in weakness meant something to them. Christianity offered them not only understanding but a social context in which they would be accepted for what they were as persons.

In general the Corinthians who believed the gospel were representative of the different social strata in the city, with the exceptions of the very top (the great magnates) and the very bottom (the mine and field slaves). They also reflected the best side of the ethos of the dynamic city. They worked on being Christians with the same commitment and enthusiasm that they brought to the other facets of their successful lives. Unlike the Galatians who were paralyzed by prudence, the Corinthians willingly accepted the responsibility of finding out for themselves what being a Christian meant in practice.

Paul stayed in Corinth for a year and a half. Shortly before his departure in September A.D. 51, Jews dragged him before Lucius Iunius Gallio, the proconsul of the Roman province of Achaia, but the charges were dismissed.

Between Corinth and Ephesus

PAUL SAILED FOR Antioch from Cenchreae, the eastern port of Corinth. His first port of call was Ephesus, where he left Prisca and Aquila to prepare the ground for his return. He had decided that the capital of the Roman province of Asia would be the place best suited for him to keep in touch with the Church communities he had founded. It was roughly in the center of a circle that encompassed them all.

From Antioch Paul went to Jerusalem to negotiate the question of whether converts to Christianity from paganism needed to be circumcised (Galatians 2:1–10). The decision went in his favor but he lost the next battle, which was to preserve the tolerant unity of the Church at Antioch. Paul felt that he could no longer belong to, or represent, a Church that discriminated against Gentile believers, forcing them in effect to become Jews (Galatians 2:11–14).

Paul left Antioch in the spring of A.D. 52, as soon as the snow in the passes to the high country had melted, and reached Ephesus by the end of that summer. Shortly before he arrived, Apollos, a convert Jew from Alexandria, sailed for Corinth with the blessing of Prisca and Aquila. The two to three years that Paul spent in Ephesus were perhaps the busiest and most productive of his life. His delegates founded churches in the hinter-land. He wrote Galatians and, during an imprisonment of uncertain dura-tion, Colossians, Philippians, and Philemon.

The Writing of 1 Corinthians

THE EVENTS THAT obliged Paul to write 1 Corinthians began in April or May A.D. 54. A wealthy woman of Ephesus, Chloe, sent some of her employees to Corinth on business. While there they frequented the Chris-tian community and were profoundly shocked at some of the things they saw. Naturally, when they returned to Ephesus they related their experi-ences.

Paul could hardly believe that practices so much at variance with the vision of Christianity that he had tried to impart had become current at Corinth. He would have liked to think that Chloe's people had misunder-stood, but the matter was too serious to push aside. It was imperative to check out their story. He sent his best assistant, Timothy, to report on the situation of the Corinthian community.

As not infrequently happens, while Timothy was on his way to Corinth, a delegation from Corinth arrived in Ephesus. His journey was no longer necessary. The delegation provided all the answers to Paul's questions. Moreover, they brought a letter informing Paul of a series of issues that were causing dissension in the community.

Paul could no longer defer writing to Corinth. He brought in Sosthenes as co-author in the belief that his intimate knowledge of the affairs of the Corinthian community would make communication easier, but quickly realized that their styles were incompatible, and in fact used him very little.

The Organization of 1 Corinthians

WHAT APPEARS TO be a complete lack of organization in 1 Corinthians has so impressed some scholars that they consider the letter to be a series of originally independent letters that a copyist strung together. The major-ity of commentators, however, rightly reject this hypothesis. Nothing in 1 Corinthians demands such radical surgery.

The seeming fragmentation of 1 Corinthians is due to the fact that Paul deals with a vast array of subjects that have been thrust upon him. He is not writing a rather abstract treatise that he was free to develop in his own way. He is reacting to urgent and divisive questions raised by a number of sources. Nonetheless the material in 1 Corinthians is not at all as disorganized as would appear at first sight.

1. Introduction (1:1–9).
2. Divisions in the Community (1:10–4:21).
3. The Importance of the Body (5:1–6:20).
4. Responses to Corinthian Questions (7:1–14:40).
    (a) Problems of Social Status (7:1–40).
    (b) Problems Arising from the Pagan Environment (8:1–11:1).
    (c) Problems in the Liturgical Assembly (11:2–14:40).
5. The Resurrection (15:1–58).
6. Conclusion (16:1–24).

The arrangement reveals a refined sense of priorities and a knowledge of how to construct an effective argument according to the principles of rhetoric. The two most important issues were divisions in the community and the resurrection. These touched the very basics of Christianity. Paul deals first with divisions in the community but saves the resurrection for the very end. A rhetorical discourse should end with a bang, not with a whimper. It should not just taper away. The most powerful arguments should be assembled and hammered home; this is a precise description of Paul's treatment of the resurrection. Other points of lesser importance are dealt with in the middle of the letter. The experts in rhetoric called this arrangement "Homeric" because of Homer's description of the battle dispositions on the plain before Troy: "Nestor put his charioteers with their horses and cars in the front; and at the back a mass of first-rate infantry to serve as the rear guard. In between he stationed his inferior troops, so that even shirkers would be forced to fight" (*Iliad* 4:299).

Although the first two chapters of Galatians are the most explicitly autobiographical material that Paul wrote, they do not reveal a fraction of what he unconsciously betrays in 1 Corinthians. The passion inspired by the variety of problems with which he has to deal in this letter force to the surface aspects of his personality that never appear elsewhere. The extraordinary ability of the Corinthians to misunderstand him provokes an intense emotion which acts as a prism that refracts in vivid colors hidden facets of his complex nature. Without 1 Corinthians we would know very little of the real Paul of Tarsus.

1 CORINTHIANS

THE GREETING

IMAGINE THE ARRIVAL of a letter from Paul in one of his communities. It was already a minor miracle for it to have reached its destination safely. Another would be necessary to achieve its desired impact on the community.

Finding the Addressees

IN A WORLD where streets had no names, and houses no numbers, the messengers—unless they were returning to their hometown—certainly had difficulty in finding the recipients. There were no church buildings that stood out from their neighbors. Christians met in homes, so Paul must have directed his letter-carriers to an individual house or apartment. We do not know how good Paul's visual memory was, but even if he gave precise directions there was no guarantee that the landmarks he recalled still existed. Business premises regularly changed hands. The tavern on the corner might now be a bakery. A grocery store could have taken the place of a restaurant. Even if the messengers found their way to the correct address, there might be no one at home. Like everyone else, believers occasionally moved, sometimes because of a chance to ascend the social scale, sometimes through necessity. With great regularity houses collapsed or were burned down.

Such problems highlight the extent to which Paul was forced to trust those who agreed to carry a letter for him, and hint at the anxiety with which he awaited a sign that his letter had been received. Irresponsible messengers might have made no effort. Conscientious ones might have failed. Fortunately, he knew that everything did not depend on him. He believed that the Holy Spirit was active among his converts, and that they were responsible for their own lives.

Insight, Not Obedience

YET AS THE one who had begotten them in Christ, Paul could not stand aside as they struggled to discern the will of God. Their previous religious beliefs, their inherited social attitudes, their relations with others in the community, all led to greatly differing perceptions of what God required of them. Amid such confusion Paul felt that he had a role to play. It was not to tell believers what God required; ready-made answers would keep them in a childish state, and he wanted them to be mature. His goal as a pastor was to promote not slavish obedience but independent insight. All he could do was to challenge them when they were going wrong, and to nudge them gently in the right direction.

Part of a Wider Movement

THE PARADOX OF the local Christian community is that it is both a whole and a part. It is independent in that the Holy Spirit guarantees it all the gifts necessary for its development. In this sense it needs nothing from outside. Yet it is also a facet of a much greater reality. Each local church is an incarnation of the ideal preached by Jesus. It gives continuing reality to the fact that Jesus is the power and the wisdom of God. This quality, however, is shared by all churches. Each, then, must hold much in common with others if the unity of the Jesus movement is to be real.

Each community, therefore, has both vertical and horizontal dimensions, both of which are channels of divine communication. The Corinthians were very conscious of the action of the Spirit among them. Their awareness of this privilege, however, expressed itself in a sense of superiority, which threatened to isolate them. Other Christians, they felt, had nothing to teach them. Thus, at the very beginning of the letter, Paul has to remind them of his broad mandate, and of the fact that there are others in many places who also call on the name of the Lord Jesus.

PRAYER

O God, make us conscious of the action of the Holy Spirit in others
as we thank you for the gifts with which we have been endowed.

THANKSGIVING

FOR PAUL EACH of his communities was a thing of wonder. Not because they were perfect, but simply because they existed. His heart was filled with gratitude for what God had done through him.

Power in Weakness

PAUL WAS A Jew in a world in which Jews were a despised minority. He was an artisan in a world that respected only intellectual achievement. He was a stranger in a world where connections were the root of power. In the face of such odds he should have achieved nothing, and he was fully aware of the fact.

Like Jeremiah, Paul could not understand why God had chosen him for a mission for which he had no built-in advantages. He had neither wealth nor social status. Unlike the prophet, however, Paul never begged to be discharged from his task. He might be unqualified, but results appeared. People turned from idols to the one true God. Christian communities came into being.

The yawning abyss between what he was and what he achieved became for Paul the key to understanding God's purpose in his calling. He knew perfectly well that every effect must have a proportionate cause. The discrepancy between his "weakness" and his churches, therefore, must be only an apparent one. Those who found his resources inadequate to explain his accomplishments should be forced to recognize that another power was at work. Paul's "weakness" made the grace of God *visible*. If Paul saw it, others should find it equally obvious. No other apologetic was necessary. God could be seen to be at work in history.

Thus, when Paul thought of the believers in the city of Corinth, whose materialism should have made any religious foundation impossible, his first reaction was gratitude, and this is why a thanksgiving is the first element in the letter. It was a moment of reassurance in a life full of stress and turmoil. The God who at times seemed distant and silent was tangibly present in his grace.

Careful Compliments

THE CORINTHIANS, OF course, had made their contribution to the miracle. They had welcomed the grace of which Paul was the channel. The change in their lifestyle was the effect of its power. Any eradication of the selfishness characteristic of life under the power of sin was an occasion for rejoicing.

But there were changes and changes. Some were more profound and far-reaching than others. Here Paul compliments the Corinthians on the profusion of spiritual gifts that they enjoy, but the gifts that he singles out for special mention are "speech" and "knowledge." These will be discussed in greater detail elsewhere in the letter—"knowledge" in chapter 8 and "speech" in chapter 14—where it will become apparent that they did not rate very highly in Paul's scale of values. They lent themselves too easily to selfish misuse. Given for the good of the Church, they were used to enhance social status in the community.

The virtues that Paul wanted to find among his converts were the fundamentals, on which he congratulates the Thessalonians: "Your work of faith, and labor of love and steadfastness of hope in our Lord Jesus Christ" (1 Thessalonians 1:3). It was these that made the Thessalonians an exemplary community, whose mere existence was a proclamation of the gospel (1 Thessalonians 1:6–8).

Paul's discretion here betrays a certain sadness. The Church at Corinth was not living up to his expectations, which, as always, were essentially missionary. The Corinthians did not offer the existential "testimony of Christ" that the world needed. They might speak of Christ, but they did not enable others to see and hear him in their behavior. They did not exhibit the "common union" *(koinonia)* among themselves and with Jesus, which is the antithesis of the divisions that characterize the world.

PRAYER

O God, enable us to live in such a way as to make your
grace a present reality in our world, so that those deafened by
words may see Christ on earth.

RIVALRY

LIFE IN THE Church and life in society were, for Paul, the two options open to humanity. The difference between the two cannot be exaggerated. One was the antithesis of the other. A decisive choice was imperative. And the Corinthians had not made it.

A World Torn Apart

PAUL WAS AN effective missionary because he had a very clear idea of the reality of the society in which he had to operate. His human world was characterized above all by divisions. Jews and Gentiles had inherited their mutual animosity, as had slaves and freemen (Galatians 3:28). But these blocks were not homogeneous. The lists of vices scattered throughout the letters (e.g., Romans 1:29–31; 1 Corinthians 5:10–11; 6:9–10) help us to look beneath the surface.

In them Paul highlights social attitudes which make genuine communication impossible. Other people were seen as a threat, with the result that individuals lived in separate compartments, cut off from others by barriers of fear and suspicion. Such isolation facilitated the propagation of the sin of "covetousness" (Romans 7:7). Energy was focused on the possession of things. Even though his language is very different, Paul is describing the loneliness and materialism of our society.

The Bond of Unity

IF DIVISION CHARACTERIZED society, unity should be the distinguishing mark of the Christian community. The dominant image used by Paul to convey the distinctive nature of the Church was that of the human body (1 Corinthians 10:17; 12:12). He also spoke of it as an olive tree (Romans 11:24).

Both of these are living things, whose unity is organic. Their constituent parts are all different—arms are not legs, and roots are not leaves—but they share a common existence. They are what they are because they belong. A sawn-off branch or a severed limb is no longer alive. Isolation changes their very natures.

Paul may have been brought to this very careful choice of images by his visits to healing temples in Asia Minor and Greece. Their walls were covered with replicas of bodily parts, which were offered by grateful patients to celebrate the power of the god. It did not take a great leap of the imagination for Paul to see the parallel between individuals in society and these replicas. Both were travesties of what they should be. An arm was truly an arm only when it formed part of a body. People were truly alive only when they belonged to a community.

Party Factions

IT SHOULD NOW be obvious why the first problem that Paul deals with in this letter is the lack of unity among the Corinthians. It was the most fundamental failure that he could imagine, and he was profoundly shocked. Their selfish attitude contradicted the most distinctive feature of the Church. What should have been a challenge to society was transformed into its accomplice. The bond of life-giving love had given way to the barriers of death. The Church could no longer fulfill its salvific mission.

To underline the seriousness of the matter, Paul asks the Corinthians if they realize that they have split up Christ. This unusual use of "Christ" to mean the community was intended to shock the Corinthians into recognizing that the Church is Christ in the world. Christ must be alive in their love in order to be active in society. A dismembered Christ can do nothing.

Acceptance of worldly standards in any sphere of Christian life is disastrous. In Paul's own case, to use the verbal tricks of professional orators in the proclamation of the gospel would be to empty the cross of Christ of its salvific power. Ministers do not create grace but they can nullify it.

PRAYER

O God, let not my pride in judgment or principle contribute to divisions within the Church. May I recognize that to be is to belong, and to accept that it is my love that helps to make Christ real in the world.

THE CRUCIFIXION COMPROMISED

AS RELIGIONS GO, Christianity is the most unreasonable. It proclaims that a crucified criminal is the savior of the world. Today's Christians cannot appreciate the incredulous revulsion which was the normal reaction to the proclamation of the gospel in the first century. Both Jews and Greeks agreed that the idea of a crucified savior was a scandal and a folly (1:23).

Believers today have never assisted at a crucifixion. Nor do they permit representations that might reflect the horrible reality. It was four hundred years before Christians used the cross as a symbol. A further two hundred years were necessary to put a figure on the cross. Only in the Middle Ages was the indescribable pain of Jesus represented graphically. Such realism did not last very long. It was too disturbing!

Crucifixion

A MORTAL SAVIOR was already extraordinary, a crucified one completely bizarre. Crucifixion was the most gruesome punishment in the ancient world. The victim was always tortured severely before being nailed to the cross in any way that satisfied the perverted whims of sadistic executioners. The pain was excruciating. Cicero perfectly conveyed the horror that crucifixion inspired by describing it as "the most cruel and disgusting penalty." It was "the most wretched of deaths" (Josephus) because at best it identified the victim as a slave, and at worst as a violent, dangerous criminal. Could such a person really be the savior of the world? To speak to anyone in the ancient world of a "savior" as "crucified" was to contradict oneself.

Benign Neglect

NOT SURPRISINGLY, THEREFORE, Paul's contemporaries played down the crucifixion. They could not deny it, but neither did they have to emphasize it. They preferred to speak merely of the death of Jesus without saying how it happened. The creed that Paul cites in 1 Corinthians 15:3–5 is typical: "Christ died for our sins according to the scriptures and was buried."

Paul saw such discreet silence as a compromise that pandered to the desire of believers to be respectable in the eyes of the world. They wanted a religious system of which they could be proud. They wanted coherent teaching that could be presented convincingly and defended rationally. They were prepared to be different, but not to be absurd. For Paul such believers had to choose between comfort and Christ. They could not have both.

God's Ways Are Not Our Ways

A CRUCIFIED SAVIOR defies logic. No arguments can make the concept palatable or intelligible. The moment the gospel is made intellectually persuasive, "the cross of Christ is emptied of its power" (1:17). Any attempt to insert the gospel into a generally accepted framework is to distort it. The conventions of society cannot determine the content of the gospel.

Once they have accepted a crucified savior, believers are forced to look on their world in a completely new way. No longer can they take for granted conventional "wisdom," namely the standards and expectations of those around them. The "wisdom of the world" could only give rise to a revelation tailored to what its supporters were prepared to accept. The desire for miracles can be made to look very religious but in reality it is an expression of skepticism. It links commitment to security, refusing the risk of trust.

Those who make the leap of faith recognize that the Crucified is the wisdom and power of God (1:24). In his total selflessness Christ exhibits God's intention for humanity. "He died for all that those who live might live no longer for themselves" (2 Corinthians 5:15). Such love is the power that transforms believers from "those who are perishing" into "those who are being saved."

PRAYER

*O God, grant that I may recognize and defeat those forces within me
that refuse the cross. Give me the strength to be crucified with Jesus and
thus be another Christ to my world.*

CLASS STRUCTURES

EVEN THOSE WHO believe in private revelations often have trouble with the recipients. Why is such a privilege so often given to children (at Fatima) or uneducated young adults (at Medjugorje) in backward areas (such as Knock in Ireland)? Their credibility is always dubious and their ability to communicate limited. Would it not be more effective and economical for God to offer revelation to those who can speak with authority and have access to the media?

The mere fact of such questions, not to mention the answers that all would give them, underlines how similar we are to the Corinthians, and how insensitive we have been to the central message of the gospel.

Transparent Instruments

IN THE PREVIOUS paragraph of this letter Paul poured scorn on the assumption of humanity that it was entitled to judge the type of revelation that God should give. According to Paul, in order to mock such "wisdom," God did something really foolish. He decided to save humanity by means of a crucified criminal!

In order to confirm that God always does the unexpected, Paul draws the attention of his readers to the make-up of their community. "Look around you," he says. "The social mix of your church contradicts what your common sense would have dictated." Paul's homely realism and his instinct for the simple, telling argument is nowhere more manifest.

The levers that nudge society in one direction or another are thought to be in the hands of those with power, position, and influence. "They" run the economy. "They" set the standards. "They" determine who succeeds and who fails. Yet such people were in the minority in the Christian community at Corinth. And this was by God's design. He had chosen otherwise.

The responsibility for the spread of the gospel rested on the shoulders of those who had few or no social advantages. In this, God was not only consistent with his choice of a savior but he made his power visible. If those who society dismissed as "nothing" were effective in founding new communities, their power must come from a source outside themselves (see 2 Corinthians 4:7). The word of God is spoken most persuasively by those who have no voice. The word of life is held out most appealingly by those who have no hands.

Those who recognize that their personal contribution is virtually nil will not take pride in their achievements. Any boasting must be a recognition of the power of God. It is from him that we truly exist through Christ Jesus.

The Ill at Ease

THE WORKING OF grace is often a mystery, but at times we are given enough hints to see how it operates. This was the case at Corinth.

As tentmakers, Prisca and Aquila had a much-needed skill, but they were Jews from a barbarian land (Acts 18:1–3). Phoebe of Cenchreae was independently wealthy, but a woman (Romans 16:1–2). Achaicus had done well enough abroad to return to Corinth as a man of leisure, but he had once been a slave (1 Corinthians 16:17). Erastus had achieved Roman citizenship, but he had begun his career in public life as a freedman (Romans 16:23).

All of these fitted awkwardly into their world. Their estimate of their own worth did not coincide with that of their contemporaries. They felt that an unflattering portrait was always imposed on the reality. Though classified as "weak" in one way or another, they knew their own power. Thus they were attracted by a message which focused on power embodied in weakness (2 Corinthians 12:9), as exemplified by a crucified savior. The gospel embodied the tension they felt within themselves. It gave meaning to their lives.

PRAYER
O God who chooses the weak, grant that I may be an effective instrument of your saving plan.

POWER PREACHING

WHAT IS THE difference between a good sermon and a bad one? Answers will differ widely. Length is one criterion, presentation another. Some will look for exegetical ability, others for current political issues. For the majority of churchgoers a sermon is good if the topic is intelligently presented with a touch of humor and contemporary relevance. The topic may have little to do with the gospel, and the pleasure is purely intellectual. The congregation will go away better informed, but not necessarily better Christians. A pleasant exercise has whiled away another Sunday morning.

Paul was much more demanding. An authentic sermon made God's saving grace *visible* by touching the hearts of the hearers with power. He believed that the same is true of all ministry. Genuine ministers, whether ordained or not, give strength, whereas ministers only in name provide impersonal service.

Writing a Beautiful Sermon

THE WORLD IN which Paul lived put a premium on the spoken word. Those who could manipulate words expertly rose to the top. To be known as an excellent speaker gave one great social prestige.

Some members of the Church at Corinth felt deeply disappointed that Paul did not measure up to their expectations as a religious leader. They could not take pride in his stature as a public speaker (2 Corinthians 10:10). Was this because Paul was naturally inept or because he had been badly educated? Neither. Paul made a carefully thought out decision, which tells us a lot about what ministry should be.

Paul's natural talent with words had been honed by a first-class education in public speaking, but he refused to put it to use in the proclamation of the gospel. The reasons were many. No orator could create or justify a religious system based on a crucified savior. No matter how clever an orator's reasoning, a more subtle mind might find devastating counterarguments. A popular preacher might be superseded by someone more attractive. Persuasive words were a poor foundation for faith.

Grace Made Visible

PAUL WAS DETERMINED that the faith of the Corinthians should be rooted in a conviction that was impregnable to the attacks of reason and resistant to the slow acid of scorn. Such conviction could only be born of direct experience, the sort of experience that we have of the hardness of wood and the wetness of water. Only fakers or fools dare to challenge the knowledge based on such experience.

Faith, therefore, had to be rooted in inescapable recognition, not in rational deduction. Paul wanted his converts to experience the power of God, to *see* divine grace in action. Their reaction had to be "My God!"—a spontaneous expression of wonder, not a deliberate "I finally worked it out."

In order to achieve this result, Paul avoided any human attraction by focusing his preaching on the most difficult part of the gospel, the crucifixion of Christ. We know from another letter that he did not simply mention the horrible death that Christ endured. He used all his great rhetorical skills to make the execution scene so vivid that his audience could believe that they were spectators (Galatians 3:1). He brought it to life before their eyes.

Paul's audience should have been horrified. They should have turned away revolted. Yet something kept them there. They saw the presence of grace in the person of Paul. They were convinced beyond any shadow of doubt that the power of God had transformed him. It was a reality they could not deny. The Holy Spirit had demonstrated its power.

PRAYER

Grant that I may be at least part of the answer to those who desperately want to see the present reality of grace, not to hear more promises.

13

How Not to Run a Church

EVEN THOUGH HE had been transformed by grace into another Christ (1 Corinthians 11:1), Paul remained a thin-skinned human being. He had made a deliberate choice in the way he preached. He let his behavior speak, keeping words to a minimum. To do him harm his opponents at Corinth gave this policy a different twist. They put out the word that he was incapable of profound religious thought expressed eloquently. The way Paul preached, they suggested, was not a matter of choice but of necessity.

Bad Ecclesiastical Leadership

UP TO THIS point in the letter, Paul had attempted to deal objectively with this criticism. He did his best to explain the reasoning behind the way he preached. His pride, however, had been pricked, and the wound festered. Gradually the infection of insult spread throughout his system. Emotion eventually overwhelmed his common sense. His opponents, Paul came to believe, were absolutely wrong. Nothing good was to be said for them. Without even questioning their hopes and desires, Paul lashed out in brutally dismissive mockery. This was a perfect example of ecclesiastical leadership at its worst.

Knowing that the intellectuals at Corinth, who despised his form of leadership, were a minority in the community, Paul decided to turn them into figures of fun. He held them up to ridicule. The cruel laughter of the majority was to be the definitive put-down.

The intellectuals may have been rather pompous, and were certainly pretentious in their claim to possess a superior wisdom, but they did not deserve the treatment they got at the hands of Paul. He did not try to understand them. He did not attempt to re-educate them. Not only was his attitude unhelpful, it was most un-Christian. And he paid a price. Even those who were unsympathetic to the intellectuals felt that Paul had gone too far. They began to question his judgment, and their support could no longer be taken for granted. The intellectuals themselves were deeply offended. In the years to come, their bitter resentment of Paul continuously thwarted his direction of the Church.

God's Secret Wisdom

THE KEY ELEMENT in Paul's strategy for dealing with the intellectuals at Corinth was to take their language and turn it inside out. He gave terms like "wisdom" and "perfect," which they cherished, a completely different meaning. He wanted them to be disconcerted when the letter was read in public (cf. Colossians 4:16). He anticipated the sniggers and nudges of the audience as the surprised intellectuals turned to each other in bewilderment. The words were theirs, but the meaning was not.

The "wisdom" the intellectuals prized was a collection of religious insights that in their view put them at the forefront of theological development. Paul dismissed it as street talk—nothing profound, nothing sensational. They had missed the point completely. True "wisdom," he insisted, could not be achieved by the use of reason alone. It could only be accepted as a divine gift. And Paul rubbed their noses in their ignorance.

Had society truly possessed wisdom, would it have been so stupid as to crucify Christ? Would it have done the one thing that guaranteed its ruin? Paul here uses the "Lord of Glory" to identify Christ. This is again the language of the intellectuals. They could not fit a suffering savior into their rational framework. As a result they tended to ignore the Jesus of history—their dismissive behavior treated him as if he were a "curse" (12:3)—and focused exclusively on the risen Lord, who of course was the sort of superior being that humanity expected as a savior.

PRAYER
God, grant that I may never use what power I have to humiliate others.

TURNING THE KNIFE

PAUL HAD NOT finished with the intellectuals at Corinth. His game of cat and mouse was not even halfway through. He had worried and confused them by his appropriation of their key term "wisdom," and by associating the "Lord of Glory" with crucifixion, but there was more to come. They thought of themselves as "spiritual" and "perfect," refined mature adults of exquisite religious sensitivity, and looked down on other members of the church as rather childish materialists incapable of theological insight.

Such uppity individuals, in Paul's view, had to be cut down to size. His secular education had given him the skills to do it. To skin an opponent with verbal knives was part of the training of any competent orator. Paul lowers himself by adopting the tactics of a world he should have left behind.

Spirit and Spirit

"SPIRIT" CAN MEAN many different things. The spirit of a team is not the spirit of an age, and neither can be drunk. The intellectuals had not thought through their use of the term "spirit" very carefully, and Paul capitalized on their sloppiness by introducing meanings they had not reckoned on.

They believed that they had penetrated the mystery of God and that their speculations had brought them unique insights. Very ostentatiously Paul sighs with exasperation. With laborious politeness he points out that no one can know what is in our human minds unless we speak our thoughts. We have to reveal ourselves if anyone is to understand us. It should be obvious even to the most simple-minded, Paul implies, that the same is true of God. The greatest intellectual effort cannot grasp the mind of God: "No one comprehends the thoughts of God except the spirit of God" (2:11). If we know what God plans for humanity, it can only be because God has revealed it. Humility, displayed in willingness to listen to God's accredited agents—namely, Paul—is the true path to valid religious knowledge. Purely human speculation creates its own idols.

The Mind of Christ

ACCORDING TO PAUL, the difference between himself and the intellectuals was that he was open whereas they were closed. He had opened himself to revelation, whereas their conviction of their intellectual superiority had closed their minds to true religious knowledge. He, therefore, was genuinely "spiritual," while they were "unspiritual." The intellectuals must have felt that their world had been turned upside down.

If Paul is the recipient of revelation, then he alone has the inspired words to communicate "wisdom." The fact that the intellectuals do not understand him just proves how incompetent they are theologically.

After this radically un-Christian put-down, Paul concludes grandiosely "we have the mind of Christ" (2:16). Even those sympathetic to Paul must have raised their eyebrows at this. The mind of Christ was expressed in self-sacrifice: "Have this mind among you, which you have in Christ Jesus . . . who emptied himself, taking the form of a servant" (Philippians 2:5–7), a theme that Paul himself had insisted on by his emphasis on the crucifixion (1:17; 2:2). Christ's attitude was the exact opposite of Paul's attempt to score points at the expense of the intellectuals! Even apostles were not immune to self-deception.

It is not hard to work out what Paul was saying: "We should have the mind of Christ, not that of a religious philosopher." What makes Christianity distinctive is not a religious idea, but the freeing and strengthening of others through the gift of self in love.

PRAYER

God, grant that I may measure myself against the cross of Christ in order not to deceive myself as to the true nature of my Christianity.

ADAPTING TO A NEW WORLD

PAUL'S CONTEMPTUOUS ATTITUDE toward the intellectuals at Corinth was inspired not by the content of their speculations, but by the mere fact of their preference for thought rather than action. For them religion was thinking about God, whereas for Paul religion was loving your neighbor as Christ loved us. For the intellectuals a new religion implied a change of mind. For Paul it meant a new world.

Mixing the Old and the New

ONCE AGAIN PAUL attacks within the framework set up by the intellectuals. They thought of themselves as "adults" because of their superior knowledge, and dismissed others in the community as "children," who could not handle the "meat" of real intellectual discourse but were limited to easily digested "milk."

On the contrary, says Paul, it is the intellectuals who are "childish." They betray their lack of true "wisdom" by failing to object to certain features of life in the church at Corinth. Some believers were jealous of the wealth or social position of others. Quarrels were common. Different agendas were being pushed and political parties came into being.

The intellectuals exhibited no surprise at such developments. Jealousy, strife, and party factions were part of the fabric of human life. Wherever they looked, in their own country or in other nations, they saw divisions characterized by suspicion and hostility. That was the way human nature was. So they dismissed the tensions within the Church with a shrug—"It's only human!"—and turned back to their theological discussions.

This attitude infuriated Paul. The intellectuals condemned him for his unsophisticated approach to religion. Their critical intelligence, they flattered themselves, opened up new horizons inaccessible to less gifted people. Yet with respect to what was going on in the Church, the intellectuals had simply accepted the common opinion as to what was possible when people lived together. They thought of themselves as dynamic thinkers, but in fact they were both docile and passive. They were too lazy to work out that acceptance of Christ should result in social changes.

The Church Is Different From Society

PAUL COULD UNDERSTAND where the intellectuals were coming from. The vast majority of his converts were mature adults who, when they became Christians, brought with them the mental and emotional baggage that they had accumulated during a lifetime in a society corrupted by the sin of selfishness (Romans 7:7). A decision to follow Christ—the act of faith— did not automatically unseat deep-rooted opinions. Believers had set themselves on a new course, and it was up to them to develop an appropriate lifestyle.

New Christians had to become critical of what they had once taken for granted. Patterns of behavior which they saw to be incompatible with the following of Christ must be rejected. To take their place they had to devise new social structures that made real the values of the gospel. Intellectuals had a part to play in this process, but those at Corinth had opted out by focusing their intellectual energy on God. The will of God can be made anything one wants it to be. Their failure to be critical of what was going on around them introduced the worm of corruption into Christianity.

As far as Paul was concerned, believers should have realized that they had to rethink their lives. If they were followers of Christ, then they should actually imitate Christ. They should act out in their daily lives the selfless love that Christ showed. If they did, there would be no place for jealousy, strife, and party factions.

PRAYER

God, grant that the Church may cease to model itself on society.
Help me to make the love shown by Christ the standard of all my words
and deeds.

GOD'S CO-WORKERS

THE SIZE OF the church at Corinth—a minimum of forty to fifty believers—made it difficult for all to meet frequently (see on 11:17–22). It was more convenient and more comfortable to meet in small groups. This facilitated the development of differences. Paul lists four groupings (1:12), but a close reading of the letter makes it clear that only two groups had any real importance—the intellectuals who had been inspired by the teaching of Apollos, and those who had remained faithful to the teaching of Paul.

Misunderstood Teachers

APOLLOS WAS TYPICAL of the energetic missionaries who spread the gospel in the first century A.D. We are completely in the dark as to how or where the gospel touched him. He was from Alexandria in Egypt (Acts 18:24), which had very close contacts with Jerusalem. Perhaps Egyptian Jews who had gone on pilgrimage to the Holy City encountered Christians and were converted by them; perhaps Apollos caught fire from their flame, and simply had to talk about it. Paul's conversion had had the same impact on him.

Apollos arrived in Ephesus after Paul had left, but encountered the couple, Prisca and Aquila, whom he had left to establish the church there. His talents impressed the Christians with whom he came in contact. Eventually it was decided that he would be more useful in Corinth (Acts 18:26–28).

A year or so later he returned to Ephesus where he met Paul for the first time (1 Corinthians 16:12). In temperament they were very different. If the mind interested Apollos, the heart was Paul's concern. They recognized, however, that there was no significant difference in their vision of the gospel.

When word of the situation at Corinth reached Ephesus (1 Corinthians 1:12; 7:1; 16:17), both Paul and Apollos were astounded. Neither had ever imagined that his words could be so twisted. Apollos had never intended to drum up opposition to Paul; Paul had believed that his message of love had been crystal clear. As they shook their heads in despair at the ability of students to get things wrong, Paul realized that it might help to heal the divisions in the Corinthian Church if he insisted that he and Apollos were not opposed to one another. It would remove at least one point of difference between the hostile factions.

Planting and Watering

PAUL WAS CITY-BRED. If he wanted an image to define the relationship between himself and Apollos, it would have been more natural for him to draw on his own trade of tentmaking or on an urban occupation like building (as in the next section). In fact he uses the farming image of planting and watering. Elsewhere he makes a key point on the relationship between Jews and Gentile Christians by means of the image of grafting an olive tree (Romans 11:17). How many city-dwellers even today know what this involves? This fondness for country images is best explained by Paul's knowledge of the parables of Jesus, which use such imagery abundantly.

The images of planting and watering show that the contributions of Paul and Apollos to the development of the Church at Corinth were complementary. Apollos nourished the seed that Paul had sown. They were essential, however, only because God had so decided. God does not need any creature in order to give grace, but in his plan of salvation he determined that grace should be given through human instruments. Ministers, therefore, are God's co-workers.

God is not limited by his revelation. He can intervene directly at any time. Miracles do happen. Normally, however, God acts indirectly. Believers are the hands and ears of God. If they do not listen, God does not hear. If they do not act, prayers go unanswered.

PRAYER
God, make me an instrument of your grace.

STRUCTURE AND FOUNDATION

NORMALLY A BUILDING is the work of many hands. An architect draws the plans, an engineer determines the structural frame, laborers pour concrete, engineers and plumbers put in wires and pipes. Paul's point in comparing the Christian community to a building is to correct a possible misinterpretation of what he has just said.

Circumstances at Corinth forced Paul to spell out what he and Apollos had done. That might have given the impression, however, that they had done everything or that only such prominent people could or should make a contribution to the development of the Church. On the contrary, every believer shares the responsibility.

The Foundation

JESUS UNDERLINED THE importance of a solid foundation by contrasting the stability of a house built on rock and that of one built on sand (Matthew 7:24–27). A wooden shack, however, does not require the same sort of foundation as a multistory building. Similarly, there are different types of community, and each has its own appropriate foundation. The foundation of a football club, for example, is not that of a theater group.

What distinguishes the Church from all other human groupings is that it is founded on a person, Jesus Christ. This, of course, changes the meaning of "foundation." It no longer signifies something unmoving, a weight of stone or concrete. Christ is a living being who is *fundamental* to the Church. Not only did he bring it into existence, he is the source of its life (Colossians 2:19). The Church depends utterly on him, just as a building depends completely on its foundation.

At this stage Paul has in the back of his mind a vision of the Church which he will make explicit only later in the letter (cf. 12:12–26). The Church is the Body of Christ. Its role is to be the physical presence of Christ in the world. It is the instrument through which Christ acts to save.

Strictly speaking, this is what the Church should be. Unfortunately a local church often fails to achieve this ideal. Instead of being a channel of grace, the behavior of its members makes it a barrier to faith. Instead of attracting, it repels. This was the case at Corinth where jealousy, strife, and party factions reigned. To outsiders the Church looked like any of the many other clubs and associations whose members jockeyed for position and power.

The Superstructure

BELIEVERS BUILD ON the foundation of Christ by what they are in the community and what they give to the community. Paul takes it for granted that all are striving to do their best for the Church. That alone is sufficient for their salvation.

Yet he is concerned to make it clear that not all contributions are equal—"gold, silver, precious stones, wood, hay, stubble"—and that one day there will be a public test that will expose the true value of each contribution. What will be classed as gold? What will be considered stubble? Paul does not tell us. That was for his converts to work out for themselves. We face the same challenge.

Paul undoubtedly would classify as gold a self-sacrificing love modeled on that of Christ on the cross. It was the supreme gift to the community, to give all for others. The gift of prophecy (14:3) might be silver; its function was to build up, encourage, and console. Hay and stubble are almost certainly something like philosophical systems or management techniques. The former may organize and correlate the truths of the faith, while the latter facilitate administration. Both, however, derive from society, and are not integral to the gospel. They may even distract from its central feature, the love of God in Christ.

PRAYER

God, give me the insight to live in such a way as to enhance the visibility of Christ, the foundation of our lives.

A SPIRITUAL TEMPLE

IN VIEW OF his harsh criticism of the intellectuals, it is rather surprising that Paul should generously assume, as the previous section suggests, that all members of the Church at Corinth were determined to make some sort of positive contribution to the development of the community. Realism, however, quickly recovered whatever ground it may have lost. He knew that believers were capable of destroying the community. It might not be their intention, but they could behave in ways that had the same effect.

Spiritual Sacrifices

IN THE LIGHT of our present knowledge, at the time of Paul only one other group thought of themselves as a spiritual temple. These were the Essenes of Qumran, the Jewish sect that produced the Dead Sea Scrolls. They prided themselves on being the most observant of all Jews, and were fiercely critical of anyone who did not measure up to their high standard. They considered the temple in Jerusalem to be so corrupt that its worship could not be pleasing to God. In consequence, they refused to take part in such worship.

This meant that they could no longer participate in the feasts that involved offering animals in sacrifice. They needed a substitute either for animals or sacrifice or for the temple. In fact they had but one option. But they could not build another temple outside Jerusalem. That was forbidden by Jewish law. Thus the Essenes were driven to develop the idea that prayers, which could be said anywhere, were the equivalent of sacrifices. "They shall expiate guilty rebellion and sinful infidelity and procure lovingkindness upon the earth without the flesh of burnt offering and the fat of sacrifice, but the offering of the lips in accordance with the law shall be as an agreeable odor of righteousness" (*Rule of the Community* 9:4–5). But for Jews sacrifice could only be offered in the Temple. Hence the place of spiritual sacrifices (the community) must be a spiritual temple.

The Indwelling of the Holy Spirit

NONE OF THE legalism that inspired Essene theology appears in Paul. His vision is at once simpler and more profound. He saw the Church as a spiritual temple because he found in it the most distinctive feature of the Temple in Jerusalem. The Temple was the house of God, the place where God dwelt on earth. The Christian community was the dwelling place of the Holy Spirit. Therefore, any group of believers was a spiritual temple.

Moreover, at Corinth the Church was the only genuine temple. Of course the city had many temples. A number have been excavated. But they contained only statues; the gods and goddesses to which they were dedicated did not really exist. The power of the Spirit, however, was evident in the Christian community. Believers experienced the presence of God.

The spiritual temple was not an end in itself. It had to do more than just exist. As the source of divine grace for the city it had a key role to play in the sanctification of Corinth. It was set apart to radiate the holiness of God. Thus to defile the spiritual temple by inappropriate behavior was not only to negate its holiness, it frustrated the carrying out of the plan of salvation. If uncorrected, the jealousy, strife, and party factions that characterized the community would expel the Holy Spirit from Corinth. Hence the seriousness of the threat with which Paul menaces the Corinthians. God is not mocked. He will destroy those who destroy his temple. How or when would this punishment be inflicted? Paul declines to answer. It would do his opponents at Corinth no harm to sweat out the uncertainty.

PRAYER

Make us aware of the fact that we are living stones, supported and supporting, in a spiritual temple. Grant that nothing in our thoughts or deeds may take from its sanctity.

13   1 CORINTHIANS 3:18–23

DON'T KID YOURSELVES

THE ABILITY OF intellectuals to deceive themselves is probably above average. Those who are brilliant in law or literature tend to assume that their superior intelligence is also attuned to dealing with finance or administration. They are not prepared to accept their limitations, and generally the results are catastrophic. The intellectuals at Corinth were no exception.

Foolish Wisdom

THE INTELLECTUALS FLATTERED themselves on their attainments, while failing to realize that their skills were inadequate to deal with Christianity. Logic and reason are incapable of coping with a crucified savior. None of the mental boxes in which we pigeonhole our rational knowledge can contain Christ. The standards of society are of no value in understanding him. Language comes apart in our hands as we try to talk of him.

Paul has attempted to get this across several times already in this letter. He now tries once again, and, to make it easier for the intellectuals, goes over the same ground. He repeats the contrast between "wisdom" and "folly," but not in exactly the same way as in 1:18–25.

The intellectuals thought they knew what these terms meant. They could trot out the dictionary definitions to which their contemporaries subscribed. Their blind spot was that they had forgotten the teaching of the Old Testament on original sin, which Paul repeated; namely, that the society which developed these definitions was not neutral or unbiased. On the contrary, it was under the control of sin (Romans 3:9). It was fundamentally distorted, deeply flawed. Thus what it understood by "wisdom" or "folly" was not necessarily correct.

The terms not only can carry very different meanings, but, Paul insists, they do. What the world considers "wisdom" is in fact "folly," and the "folly" of society is "wisdom" as far as God is concerned.

Belonging

MANY FACTORS DIVIDED the different groups at Corinth, but for convenience they were identified by their leaders: the Apollos faction, the Paul faction, and so on (1:12). With his keen instinct for the perfect put-down Paul invents a slogan for each party: "I belong to Paul," "I belong to Apollos." In antiquity this sort of language was not used to describe political affiliation or a relationship to an esteemed teacher. It was used only when speaking of children or slaves who were identified by their relationship to their parents or masters. The effect of the slogans was to dismiss the formation of the factions as low-class childishness.

Paul here rubs salt into the wound by highlighting a contradiction in the attitude of the intellectuals. Everyone knew the popular saying "All things belong to the wise," which meant that they had total control over all that came to them from outside. Had the intellectuals at Corinth been as smart as they thought they were, they should have said "Apollos belongs to us"!

His inability to resist a chance to slide in the knife did Paul no good among his readers, but what he wanted to get across remains valid. The only reference point for Christians is Christ; to him alone do we belong. Under God he is the sole source of our new life (1:30). All leaders are only servants, or as Paul put it earlier, "instruments [in the hand of God] through whom you believed" (3:5). This reversal of normal values extends to the forces that used to control human existence—namely, the world, life, death, the present, and the future. The rhetorical sweep of the series is most impressive. The hope given in Christ liberates believers from these forces.

PRAYER

Grant that I may become a fool in the eyes of the world in order to become truly wise in Christ.

SERVING TWO MASTERS

"NO ONE CAN serve two masters!" When Jesus made this pronouncement, he drew out the consequences from the point of view of the slave: "Either he will hate the one and love the other, or he will be devoted to the one and despise the other" (Matthew 6:24). The emotional turmoil is rooted in the fact that different masters will inevitably make conflicting demands. One may give the servant the day off, while the other insists on work. One may want the servant to wear a uniform, while the other orders casual dress.

No servant could be in a more awkward position, and that is just where Paul has placed the Christian minister.

Trapped!

PAUL CERTAINLY FELT a glow of satisfaction at the neat point he had just scored by insisting that the Corinthian slogan "I belong to Paul" should really be "Paul belongs to you" (3:22). But perhaps he had been too clever by half and had let his tongue run away with him. He had proclaimed himself the servant of the community. That gave the Church the right to dictate what he should do! But he had been sent by God (1:1). He was also God's servant!

Paul had trapped himself on the horns of a dilemma. He had already implicitly refused to conform to the type of religious leadership that at least some members of the Church at Corinth expected. They wanted an orator who would do them honor in public. They desired a gospel that was logically consistent. Now by his own cleverness he had put himself in their power. Paul knew that he had the technical skills to act in the way a number of the Corinthians required. He was a fully trained orator, who knew the rules of public discourse better than they. What he could not do, however, was to replace the power of the cross by mere words (1:17).

Who Judges?

PAUL INSISTS THAT he can be challenged only by God. As a steward he is not restricted by detailed orders. He is expected to use his initiative in deciding how to communicate the gospel effectively. But he has to understand, and be faithful to, the intentions of his master. God, in consequence, is the only one competent to decide if Paul has made a mistake.

Paul's concern here is to deny to the Corinthians any right to judge him, but he is logical enough to admit that if God *alone* can judge in matters of ministry, then no human being has the right. Thus Paul cannot even judge himself! In effect he says, "Even if I am convinced that I have nothing on my conscience, there is no guarantee that God agrees" (4:4). Pride in performance is no protection against the judgment of God. "I have nothing to reproach myself with" is a hollow claim. Those who proclaim their clean consciences are sanctimonious, not saintly.

Thus, from a different starting point, Paul returns to the most fundamental principle of his apostolate. There are no detailed commandments against which we can measure our progress. All law is reduced to the commandment of love (Romans 13:8–10). And the standard of love is the self-sacrifice of Christ.

PRAYER

God, grant that I may ask, not "Is my conscience clean?" but "Have I given all that Christ gave?"

THE RESULTS OF REVERENCE

ALL AGREE THAT the text of the Bible merits reverence. If such reverence, however, is not accompanied by simple common sense the results can be catastrophic, as this single verse perfectly illustrates.

When the Bible was copied by hand mistakes were often made. The eye of a tired scribe working in poor light might confuse letters that looked alike, or he might repeat part of a word, or he might jump from a word in one line to a similar or identical word a line or two lower, thereby omitting whole phrases. Such errors were sometimes corrected without fuss by later scribes. I believe that here we have an exception. A scrupulous copyist, whose veneration for the sacred text was great, added a note explaining what he had done, and created chaos.

An Intelligent Correction

THE SCRIBE READ in the text he was copying, "I have applied all this to myself and Apollos for your benefit, believers, that you may learn from us to be puffed up in favor of one against the other." The scribe's eyes popped. This could not possibly be right. It put Paul at odds with Apollos, and encouraged the hostile parties at Corinth to feel superior with respect to each other. But this is exactly the opposite of what Paul had been trying to get across. He was not opposed to Apollos (3:5–9), and he had made it clear that factions had no place in the Church (1:13; 3:21–22).

What had gone wrong? His common sense told the scribe that one of his predecessors had accidentally omitted a "not." His veneration for the sacred text, however, immediately gave rise to a scruple. Perhaps he had not understood what Paul wanted to say! The copyist could not quite bring himself to ignore his common sense, and decided to compromise by inserting the missing "not" and adding a note to explain what he had done. This gave his readers the chance to decide for themselves.

Thus the scribe copied what he believed Paul had actually written: "I have applied all this to myself and Apollos for your benefit, believers, that you may learn from us *not* to be puffed up in favor of one against the other." In the margin he wrote, "The 'not' is above what was written." Today we might say "The text I was copying lacked the 'not.' "

Blind Reverence

THE NEXT SCRIBE to copy the corrected manuscript was not very intelligent. He did not realize that the marginal note "The 'not' is above what is written" was a comment by his predecessor. He thought that it was part of Paul's letter that had been accidentally omitted, and had then been scribbled in the margin on revision. Parchment was expensive, and there was no question of scrapping a page if a mistake had been made. The omission had to be written in wherever the scribe could find space, between the lines or in the margin. The next copyist would make it tidy again.

His blind reverence for the scriptures led the scribe to produce the text preserved in our Bibles, which, translated literally, is "I have applied all this to myself and Apollos for your benefit, believers, that you may learn not above what is written lest one be puffed up in favor of one against the other."

This is nonsense, but the reverence of translators and commentators for Paul has transformed it into mysterious profundity. It must be meaningful. Words are added at will, and "what is written" becomes variously the rules of the game, a list of regulations, or the scriptures! This is not genuine respect for the text.

PRAYER

God, grant that I may read your word with reverence, but also with an awareness of the frailty of those who served as your instruments.

SAVAGE SARCASM

PAUL REFUSED TO use his rhetorical skills in presenting the gospel
(2:1–5) because he did not want belief to rest on human arguments. He
had no scruple about using such techniques to flay his opponents. The
quality of his education is apparent in the virtuosity with which he uses
one of the most vicious weapons of an orator or writer, namely sarcasm.
The word comes from the Greek verb *sarkazo*, "to tear flesh like dogs."
This is precisely the way in which Paul treats certain members of his
flock. That he was impatient, frustrated, or disappointed is hardly an
excuse. Authentic Christian leadership should give life, not take away
dignity.

Wounding Questions

THE INTELLECTUALS AT Corinth were proud of their wisdom, and treated
those they considered their inferiors with contempt. They needed to be
corrected, but Paul opted to destroy them. He struck at the heart of their
identity as human beings. "Who," he sneered, "makes you different?"

Each individual is unique and irreplaceable. This awareness founds my
sense of self-worth. If no one is precisely like me, then I have a specific
contribution to make. I am a valuable member of society. This conviction
is the basis of my mental health, and enables me to function effectively
and to live with dignity.

This is what Paul attempted to take from the Corinthians. His questions
would have been devastating if addressed to the intellectuals in private,
but they were part of a letter to be read in public. The intellectuals were
given no place to hide as they were stripped of their self-respect.

Paul then piles insult upon injury. He smears the intellectuals as dis-
honest and ungrateful. They claimed as their own what they had in fact
received from God. They boasted as if they had achieved something when
in reality it was God's gift.

In a sense these accusations were true, but they did not represent the whole truth. Paul obviously expected his audience to remember his teaching that divine grace underlay all they had and were. For the moment he does not wish them to recall his insistence that human cooperation is essential to the operation of grace. Believers are set free only for freedom (Galatians 5:1). It is up to them to make such freedom a reality. God does not give it. Thus the intellectuals, like all believers, could claim credit for the good use made of grace. But in the heat of the moment that was far from Paul's mind.

Bitter Irony

HAVING PUT THE intellectuals in the wrong, Paul turns to mocking irony and rubs salt in their wounds by deliberately distorting what they were doing. He presents as actual achievements what for them were only hopes and dreams. To believe Paul, the intellectuals claimed to possess all spiritual gifts and to enjoy the kingdom of God. There is no evidence that they believed anything of the sort.

Paul's bitterness becomes understandable when he contrasts his sense of reality with the fantasies of the intellectuals. "We *feel* ourselves to be fools, but you *think* yourselves wise. We *feel* ourselves weak but you *think* yourselves strong. You *imagine* that you are held in honor, but we *know* ourselves to be disreputable." Those who struggle in misery find it hard to be charitable to those thought to live in complacent luxury.

PRAYER

God, grant that my sense of my own righteousness may be clothed with the humility that comes from believing that all I have and am is ultimately God's gift.

STRESS AND STRAIN

THAT PAUL FELT at least some guilt for his abuse of the intellectuals (4:7–10) is suggested by his lapse into self-pity. In order to bury the memory of what he had done to them, he focuses on what was done to him.

A Hard Life

NO ONE GAVE Paul a regular salary. He had to pay his own way. On the road he had to find money for room and board at an inn each night. Roman officials from the highest administrator to the lowest soldier could requisition what took their fancy. The result was that there was no charity anywhere on or near a Roman road. In each new town he had to find work to support himself, and a place to stay.

Each day was an agonizing balancing act. He had to earn enough to survive. But he also had to proclaim the gospel. If he gave time to speaking about Jesus during the day, he often had to work through the night (2 Thessalonians 3:8). The occasional gift of money was most welcome (Philippians 4:16), and became increasingly indispensable as his pastoral responsibilities grew.

On the Roman roads throughout Asia Minor (modern Turkey) and Greece, inns were spaced roughly twenty-two miles apart. That was a day's steady walking. As he was setting out, however, Paul might be called to repair a traveler's equipment or the tack of a carriage. He had to take the job because he needed the money, but the delay meant that he would not reach the inn before nightfall. The consequence was a cold and hungry night in the open. Or, while on the road, he might be requisitioned by a platoon of soldiers to repair their leather cloaks or sandals. A lot of work paid for by an insulting blow, and most of the daylight gone.

Robbers infested the roads. In particularly bad areas Paul would have to waste time and money waiting for a group of travelers going in his direction. In no town did Paul have the connections that guaranteed protection. He was the outsider who could be victimized with impunity. There were no police forces to which he could appeal. The military did not intervene in civil matters. In any sort of trouble, Paul was on his own. Despised and humiliated, he seethed with the impotent anger of the weak (2 Corinthians 11:29).

Repaying Evil with Good

THROUGH HIS CONVERSATIONS with Peter (Galatians 1:18), Paul knew a lot about the person and teaching of the historical Jesus. The idealism of the Sermon on the Mount had impressed him profoundly: "If anyone strikes you on the right cheek, turn to him the other also; and if anyone would sue you and take your coat, let him have your cloak as well . . . Love your enemies and pray for those who persecute you" (Matthew 5:39–44). "Bless those who curse you; pray for those who abuse you" (Luke 6:28).

This principle of love of enemies guided Paul in his response to those who looked down on him as a manual laborer (though not to those who questioned his style of religious leadership!) and to those who told lies about him. His abject failure to respond forcefully to his attackers would have lowered him even further in their eyes. His menial position was one thing, lack of courage another, whatever it might have cost him. Their standards, however, were not his. He modeled himself on Jesus, who said, "Father forgive them, for they know not what they do" (Luke 23:34).

PRAYER
Lord, grant that insult and injury may never turn me from the proclamation of the gospel in word and deed.

MY WAYS IN CHRIST

WHEN CHLOE'S EMPLOYEES returned to Ephesus from a business trip to Corinth, they regaled the community with a vivid account of some bizarre features of their sister Church (1:11). Paul was deeply disturbed, but did not know how to react to what might be only malicious gossip. Had Chloe's people really understood? Many envied the prosperity of Corinth and the skill of its traders. Had Chloe's people lost out on a deal, and were they trying to besmirch the reputation of those who had bested them? The incidents were too important to be avoided by putting trust in such possibilities. Paul had to be sure. In consequence, he decided to send Timothy, his closest friend and collaborator (Philippians 2:19–22), to find out what was going on.

After Severity, Sweetness

PARENTS WHO HAVE lost a child for several hours will best appreciate what is going on in this part of the letter. Searing anxiety is released in recriminations, which quickly give way to expressions of affection. Paul's abuse of the intellectuals (3:7–10) sprang from his anxiety for the fate of the community, but it was rooted in love.

There were two dominant figures in the life of the Corinthian community, Paul and Apollos. Earlier in the letter the image of planting and watering was used to define their relationship (3:5–9). In order to diffuse the rivalry of the different groups within the Church, Paul insisted that both he and Apollos had made indispensable contributions and that their roles were complementary.

From this some might conclude that Paul put Apollos on the same level as himself. Far from it! Paul's relation to the community was unique, whereas that of Apollos could be duplicated by any number of others. A person can have many teachers but only one father.

Paul's basis for claiming paternity of the Corinthians was not that he had gotten to know them first. There was much more to it than that. To those who were being saved the gospel was the power of God. Paul had been God's instrument in giving them "life," as the father and mother are responsible under God for the birth of a child. Prior to his arrival among them they had been "dead," inward-looking, self-centered, unloving. The power of the gospel, which he channeled to them, gave them the capacity to model themselves on Christ, who had given his life for others (2 Corinthians 5:15).

Imitation

BUT NONE OF the Corinthians had ever met Christ. They had certainly heard about him from Paul, but that is not the same thing as *seeing*. Words may describe a lifestyle that is superhuman. Only achievement shows what is really possible. The fact that no human being has ever flown unaided from one building to another shows Superman's feat to be fiction.

Thus it was pointless for Paul to tell his converts to imitate Christ. The conviction that it was genuinely possible could not be generated by even the most vivid word-picture. Only when there is real hope of success will people commit themselves fully. Thus Paul could only propose his own example: "Imitate me as I imitate Christ" (11:1). He had lived among the Corinthians for a year and a half (Acts 18:11). They knew his lifestyle. But they had forgotten its Christ-like demands, and needed to be reminded. He could do so verbally, and so could Timothy. But Paul also hoped that they would see him in his "beloved and faithful child" Timothy.

The implications for ministry cannot be too heavily emphasized. The demands of Christ can never be expressed in a list of rules, however comprehensive. They must become visible in the behavior of a Christ-like figure.

PRAYER
God, grant that I may represent Christ to others in love, compassion, and self-sacrifice.

POWER, NOT TALK

IT MUST HAVE been difficult to travel and work with Paul. The strong emotional component in his personality emerges very vividly from the mood swings that we have encountered in this chapter alone. A reasonable, moderate tone (4:1–6), gives way to savage sarcasm (4:7–10), which is replaced by brave self-pity (4:11–13), which becomes anxious affection (4:14–17), which here turns into heated warnings. Were such sudden shifts part of Paul's normal behavior, one would never know where one was with him. One would always have to walk carefully, which is very wearying.

A Threatened Visit

TIMOTHY'S MISSION TO Corinth was simply to report on the situation there. Paul gave him a second duty, namely, to represent Paul, the imitator of Christ (4:16–17). The second function was necessary because, in the interval since Timothy's departure, Paul had been made certain by the delegation from Corinth (16:17) that the Corinthians had deviated from the type of behavior that Paul considered appropriate to followers of Christ.

All of a sudden Paul realizes the implications of what he has done, and his imagination runs wild. He has dropped Timothy into a snake pit! If the intellectuals at Corinth had treated Paul with contempt, what would they do to Timothy who was younger and much less experienced? They would eat him alive. Timothy would be no match for their skill in debate, and his inability to play by their rules would be interpreted as confirmation of the weakness of Paul. Would a really competent leader have sent such an inept representative? Perhaps, they would insinuate, Paul might have taken on too much in claiming authority over the Church.

The power of Paul's imagination makes the discomfort, even danger, that Timothy might experience, and the renewed threat to his own authority, vividly real. Paul's blood boils. He lashes out with a warning that if push comes to shove he himself will come to Corinth to sort things out. It is not that far away. A fast boat from Ephesus could get him there in a week with fair winds. The Corinthians are put on notice that there will be serious trouble if anything happens to Timothy, and if they continue their sniping at Paul. No date for Paul's arrival is fixed. The uncertainty is a deliberate device to keep the Corinthians off balance.

God's Kingdom Does Not Consist in Talk but in Power

THE BASIS OF Paul's belief that he could overwhelm the intellectuals at Corinth was not his confidence in the quality of his education. He was probably a much better trained debater than they were, but he had vowed not to use those skills in the presentation or defense of the gospel (2:1–5). Equally, he was not in a position to take any type of physically repressive action against his opponents. The Roman authorities would have taken a very dim view of any such disturbance of public order.

Paul put his faith in what he was convinced was the obvious difference between the gospel and any theological or philosophical system. Philosophers and theologians were capable of drawing up detailed blueprints for human behavior, and they had been doing so for centuries. Yet they had not effected any lasting change in significant numbers of people. They produced only words. The gospel, on the contrary, had transformed the lives of those who accepted it. It embodied the power of God in history (1:18; Romans 1:16). "The kingdom of God does not consist in talk but in power" (4:20).

PRAYER
O God, the power of religious leaders derives from the gospel, grant that they may not corrupt it by confusing theological speculation with the following of Christ.

INCEST

THE CORINTHIANS WERE most unlike the Galatians. They belonged to different racial stock. The Corinthians were basically Greek, with additions from the racial spectrum of the eastern Mediterranean, whereas the Galatians were essentially Celtic with an admixture of Phrygian. The psychological difference was even greater. The Galatians were frightened of the freedom to determine their own lives. Their need to be right paralyzed them. Their prudence was so great that they took no risks. The Corinthians, on the contrary, enthusiastically took up Paul's challenge to work out for themselves what it meant to live as a Christian. Unfortunately they sometimes got it wrong!

Being Different

PAUL HAD TOLD the Corinthian Christian community that it must be as different from the rest of the city as light from darkness (Philippians 2:14–16). He expected it to realize that this meant loving others as Christ loved us. The Corinthians highlighted a different type of love. A member of the community had set up house with his stepmother.

Such a union was explicitly forbidden by both Jewish (Leviticus 18:7–8) and Greco-Roman law (Gaius, *Institutes*, 1:63). Presumably, when the couple started to live together, shock waves went through the Church. They were not only doing something immoral but they were laying themselves open to arrest. And the Church might be implicated. Then someone pointed out that to approve the arrangement would make the community unique in the city. The believers would be doing exactly what Paul had asked of them! In addition, he had warned them of the possibility of persecution.

Excommunication

THE CORINTHIANS SHOULD have seen that their approval of, and support for, the incestuous couple made the community the butt of contemptuous remarks by outsiders. Those who perceived the Church as a hotbed of immorality could not see it as the Body of Christ. The failure of believers to see the missionary implications of what they were doing, and to deal with it by expelling the offender (apparently his stepmother was not a Christian), was typical of the childishness that characterized the Corinthian Church (3:1; 14:20).

It infuriated Paul that intelligent adults could be so perverse. But he could not simply step in and tell them what to do. That would be self-defeating. If parents make all the decisions for a son or daughter, that child will never grow up mentally. Paul saw very clearly that none of his communities would produce mature Christians if he made their decisions for them. Compulsory goodness has no value (Philemon 14). While in jail, criminals commit no crimes.

If Paul found it impossible to order the expulsion of the offender, he certainly made his opinion clear. He did so in a way that is a model for the relationship of a bishop to a parish. The parish is a local church in which the bishop does not live but for which he has responsibility. Paul was dealing with Corinth from Ephesus, on the other side of the Aegean Sea. His strategy was to claim spiritual presence in the meeting at Corinth that debated the issue. This both affirmed the independence of the Church there, and gave him a voice in its affairs. He could express his opinion forcibly without predetermining the decision of the Church.

Paul's purpose was to challenge the community to purify itself, and to save the sinner by forcing him to see the error of his ways. Spending time in the cold selfishness of society should make him long for the supportive warmth and love that he had experienced in the Church.

PRAYER

God, grant that my local church may not imitate the childish blindness of the Corinthians in the face of evil, but may have the courage to purify itself from the insidious corruption of society.

SOCIAL SIN

THE IMAGE OF flat unleavened bread may have popped into Paul's mind because he was writing this letter during Passover. It was certainly not long before Pentecost (16:8), which falls fifty days after Passover. In preparation for Passover the Jewish home is scrupulously swept clean of every scrap of leaven, the ingredient that makes dough rise (Exodus 12:15–20). Leaven thus became a natural symbol for wickedness, which should be excluded from the community. The relevance to the expulsion of the incestuous man is obvious. But why would it have been wrong to keep him within the community? The answer is tied to Paul's understanding of freedom.

Under the Power of Sin

ORIGINAL SIN, AS far as Paul was concerned, operated through the force of bad example. Evil decisions over thousands of years had coalesced into a system of false values that distorted society. Individuals, for example, were valued not for who they were but for what they had. Certain forms of dishonesty, such as cheating on taxes, were treated as virtues. Those born into that society could no more avoid being influenced by such values than a chip of wood can resist the current of a river.

Without being entirely aware of it, all were forced to think and act in the same selfish manner as their neighbors. It was the way everyone lived. The power of society to bring individuals into line became apparent only when someone tried to break away from the pack. Those who protested against unjust wars or corrupt practices in business were very quickly reduced to impotence. This is the power of sin (Romans 3:9) to which humanity is enslaved (Romans 6:6).

Set Free for Freedom

HOW COULD ANYONE be freed from sin? Only by moving out of society into a group that lived by a completely different set of values, a community in which the dominant influence was good example. But was such an alternative possible?

Paul inherited from Judaism the belief that the community of the Messiah would contain no sinners. All would be just (Isaiah 60:21). Jesus, however, was the promised Messiah. Hence his Church was the sinless community. Ideally, in it everyone was uplifted by the force of good example. It was easy to love, to be generous, to be selfless, to pray, because that was the way all followers of Christ lived. The influence of bad example in society was blocked by the superior force of good example in the Christian community. Even though the Church was in the world, it did not belong to the world. It could reach out to sinners, but they could not penetrate it.

Freedom, therefore, was not something that each individual possessed separately. It was not given once and for all at conversion. It had to be consciously and continuously maintained. It grew out of the web of relationships in a community of love, and was dependent on the genuineness of these relationships. Any failure in love on the part of one member of the community put all other members at risk. They owed each other love. Selfishness diminished the protective force that held the power of sin at bay. All paid a price if this barrier was breached.

Thus there was no such thing as an entirely private sin. Every sin had consequences for others. An infected finger, if not attended to, will spread its poison throughout the body. The incestuous man had to be expelled if the Body of Christ was to be healthy and free.

PRAYER

Lord, do not permit me to take freedom for granted, and make me ever aware that my love for others is part of their freedom.

A Convenient Misunderstanding

IDEALISTIC AS PAUL was in his belief in the sinlessness of the Church, he was intensely realistic regarding what actually went on in his communities.

The Baggage of the Past

PAUL KNEW PERFECTLY well that all believers were not sinless. He was fully aware that the act of faith in Jesus Christ did not in itself destroy the deep-rooted selfish habits that his adult converts brought with them into the Church.

Ways of thinking and acting that put an individual at the center of a private universe had been part of his converts' normal pattern of behavior for twenty or thirty years. The struggle for survival had made looking out for number one the highest priority. In the Church that attitude had to be abandoned. Others were to be esteemed above oneself. Believers had to learn how to love.

All that Paul demanded of them was that they try hard. He did not look for total success. In fact he doubted that such perfection was possible (Philippians 3:12–16). Consistent effort, on the other hand, was imperative. Otherwise they were only nominally followers of Christ, and their freedom from sin was a fantasy. The promises of the gospel had to be made real by actually loving one's neighbor.

Lazy Corinthians

PAUL HAD EXPLAINED all this to the Corinthians but, if they listened, they certainly had not understood. Only one aspect of the gospel had retained their attention: They had been saved by a risen Lord. They refused to accept that what was true in theory had to be made true in fact. Thus they set aside Paul's insistence that they had to change. The way they did it was rather clever. They made Paul appear to have demanded the impossible.

Paul had told the Corinthian Christians not to associate with "immoral people." He meant those who had drifted into the new Church out of curiosity and without any great commitment, as well as those who had started well but who had found the incessant effort too much. The incestuous man was typical of such people who dragged believers back to their preconversion status. His own pleasure outweighed the needs of others.

It is probable that Paul did not spell out these qualifications. He tended to assume that his audience knew what he meant to say, and then got upset when they drew the opposite conclusions from what he intended. Other instances of this occur in the letter.

The Corinthians understood "immoral people" as meaning the unconverted members of society. Such people were all around in Corinth, and in all other countries. The only way to avoid them would be to go to live on another planet. Paul, they said, could not really have demanded anything so ridiculous. Hence, they concluded, it would be kinder to pass over in silence all his absurd statements about not associating with immoral people. Paul did not know what he was talking about.

Apollos reported this bizarre interpretation when he returned to Ephesus (16:12). As might be expected, Paul was profoundly disturbed, not only by what he saw as the deliberate distortion of what he had said, but by the consequences for the Church. If the Corinthian view prevailed, no standards could be enforced in the community. It would inevitably degenerate into one of the many secular associations that formed part of the social fabric of Corinth. It would no longer be the Body of Christ. Believers would lose their freedom. Hence, he insisted, those who will not try to love must be expelled.

PRAYER

God, grant that we may not deceive ourselves in interpreting the demands of the gospel. May the following of Christ be our sole aid in discerning the will of God.

WASHING DIRTY LINEN

THE TIME LAG between the moment of conversion and the corresponding change in behavior is perfectly illustrated by the fact that the Corinthians continued to use civil courts to iron out problems in their business relationships. They had committed themselves to an entirely new way of life in Christ, but continued to maintain the conventions of society. They took it for granted that the legal means used by their pagan neighbors to seek redress for their grievances was the only one. The believers had forgotten the need to forge a new pattern of behavior that proclaimed the Church's difference from all other groups.

A Bitter Dispute

THE SPECIFIC PROBLEM that drew Paul's attention to the way the Corinthians went about their business affairs appears to have been a case of fraud. One member of the community cheated another, causing him or her a financial loss. If the matter was brought before a court the sum must have been considerable, and the adversaries wealthy. Thus the parties were socially prominent, and possibly leaders in the Church.

The affair was reported to Paul by Chloe's employees (1:11). Being business people they were used to such cases, and took them for granted. There must have been something unusual about this particular trial that made the Ephesians remember it. One might not be far wrong in suspecting a depth of bitterness that found expression in some very nasty mudslinging. This revelation of the total lack of love among those who were supposed to be brothers and sisters was what scandalized Chloe's people. The complacency of other members of the Church made matters worse. They felt no need to intervene. One can see the shrug of the shoulders and hear the comment "That's human nature!"

Overcoming Obstacles

THIS FURTHER EVIDENCE that the Corinthians had not the faintest idea of what Christianity was really about infuriated Paul, and with cold venom he attacks the intellectuals. With good reason he saw them at the root of most of the problems that beset the Church. If they were so clever, Paul says, why did they not put their superior intelligence to good use by dealing with the case within the community? If they looked down on fellow Christians, they must despise non-Christians. Why then would they trust them as judges?

Such language might give the impression that Paul thought that Christians should have their own courts to settle such disputes within the community. Christians could then throw mud at each other, and none of it would reach the outside world. The Church would appear to be squeaky clean, no matter what went on behind closed doors. This certainly was not Paul's solution.

In principle, he maintained, there should be no lawsuits among Christians. Why? They are all members of the Body of Christ. For one to sue another is as idiotic as an arm suing its own leg. Can one sue oneself? Once again the Corinthians had failed to think through the implications of the gospel they had accepted.

If disputes did arise, they should be taken as opportunities to demonstrate the power of love. For Paul, every quarrel between believers was a chance to impress neighbors who would see a community with the same problems as the rest of the world resolve those problems in a radically different way. It was unfortunate if one Christian fell out with another, but love becomes most visible in situations where the world presumes it should not exist at all. Tranquillity has an impact only when it is known to be a triumph. Success must be a surprise to scintillate.

PRAYER

O God, let us pray, not for a peaceful community but for the wisdom and love to transform the inevitable quarrels into a proclamation of the presence of divine love here and now.

BEFORE AND AFTER

PAUL MUST HAVE felt a certain satisfaction in the way he had held up a mirror to the Corinthians so that they could see the contradiction in which they had trapped themselves. He was aware, however, that subtle arguments were not always the most effective with this particular group of believers. If they could misunderstand what he considered (not always correctly) perfectly plain statements, anything less straightforward might go right by them. Hence, he had to make them realize that baptism had been a watershed in their lives. There was a before and an after, and each had its own appropriate way of acting.

Before Conversion

FOR PAUL, LIFE without Christ was characterized above all by division. An overview of the world revealed hostile blocs: Jew against Gentile, master against slave, male against female (Galatians 3:28). These were bitterly opposed to one another. When Paul looked closely at each of the groups the picture was even less pleasant. The members were not united. They were separated by barriers of fear and suspicion. This picture emerges from a whole series of lists of vices, of which 6:9–10 is one. The others are Romans 1:29–31; 13:13; 1 Corinthians 5:10–11; 2 Corinthians 12:20–21; Galatians 5:19–21; and Colossians 3:5, 8. When the overlaps are discounted we are left with forty-one vices, the vast majority of which are antisocial in the sense that they make genuine communication impossible. The list here is typical of others.

In context "wrongdoing" refers to the case of fraud (6:8); once cheated, ever mistrustful. "Fornication" evokes the sort of casual sex in which the other is treated merely as an object of pleasure (6:15). "Adultery" deeply wounds the deceived partner. "Thieves" and "robbers," motivated by "greed," not only cause loss but sow insecurity and suspicion. "Drunkards" are self-centered, insensitive to the needs of others. The abusive "slanderer" poisons the social atmosphere with lies. In a world populated by such people it is easy to see how individuals are forced into isolation: It paid to be selfish; to reach out to others was likely to have disastrous consequences.

There are two other terms in this list, the passive and active partners in a male homosexual relationship. At first sight these do not seem to fit with the other vices because sometimes homosexual relationships are models of enduring affection. In reality, however, the terms suggest an effeminate young male prostitute who is used by an older sodomite. This was the most common form of homosexuality in the ancient world, and was viciously exploitative on both sides. Thus for Paul it typified the degenerate relationships that characterized society.

After Conversion

PAUL'S VISION OF the world in which he lived was the fruit of hard experience. And only a fool would deny its truth. The need to survive meant continuous pressure to conform, to put self before others. He recognized that he could maintain his ideal of total commitment to others only because he was protected by the love of the community.

The Corinthians benefited in the same way. Despite their many failures, there had been some successes. Even though the community had a long way to go, believers had changed to some degree. After they were washed in the water of baptism and anointed with the Holy Spirit there had been a movement of cooperation on their part, which had led to greater generosity in their relationships with others. A more serious effort, however, was necessary if they were not to slide back into the dog-eat-dog world from which they had come.

PRAYER

God, make me ever aware that the warmth of those who love me is all that protects me from the chill winds of selfishness. Help me to assure them the same protection.

DIALOGUE AT LAST!

PAUL DID NOT write because it gave him pleasure. Each letter had to be forced out of him by a crisis that demanded his intervention. A letter, in consequence, gives us only one half of a dialogue. Reading it is like being in a room with a friend on the phone. We hear only one side of the conversation, and have to guess what the person at the other end of the line is saying. Occasionally a few words come through when the phone is not tightly clamped to our friend's head. Immediately what they are talking about becomes clearer.

Reconstructing the Conversation

JUST AT THIS point in the letter we begin to hear snatches of what the Corinthians are saying. For the first time there is no guesswork in determining to what Paul is responding. We know not only what Paul says but why he says it.

The conventions of writing at the time of Paul differed from ours. In particular, quotations were not marked by inverted commas or indentation. Thus nothing in any ancient manuscript of 1 Corinthians tells us that a phrase was spoken by the Corinthians. Nonetheless we can sometimes tell that it was, because in the letter we find statements with which Paul disagrees. This leaves us with two choices. Either he changes his mind in the middle of a sentence, or he is contradicting someone else. Since the first is highly unlikely, we must choose the second. So let us set out 6:12–20 as if it were a script for a play, using the text of the New Revised Standard Version. Stage directions can be added according to taste.

The Dialogue

CORINTHIANS: All things are lawful to me.
PAUL: But not all things are beneficial.
CORINTHIANS: All things are lawful to me.
PAUL: But I will not be dominated by anything.

CORINTHIANS: Food is meant for the stomach and the stomach for food, and God will destroy both one and the other.

PAUL: The body is meant not for fornication, but for the Lord, and the Lord for the body. And God raised the Lord and will also raise us by his power.

Do you not know that your bodies are members of Christ? Should I therefore take the members of Christ and make them members of a prostitute? Never!

Do you not know that whoever is united to a prostitute becomes one body with her? For it is said, "The two shall become one flesh" [Genesis 2:24]. But anyone united to the Lord becomes one spirit with him. Shun fornication!

CORINTHIANS: Every sin that a person commits is outside the body.

PAUL: On the contrary, the fornicator sins against the body itself. Do you not know that your body is a temple of the Holy Spirit within you, which you have from God, and that you are not your own? For you were bought with a price; therefore glorify God in your body.

Once the text is laid out in this way it becomes clear how far apart Paul and the Corinthians were on fundamental issues. Paul is content to tone down the slogan about complete freedom to do what one likes, but he disagrees forcefully with their view that, as far as morality is concerned, the human body is completely irrelevant. We must now look more closely at both sides of the debate.

PRAYER

Lord, when I am involved in theological discussion, grant that I may listen to others with sympathy for what they are trying to express, and that I may voice my own views with moderation and modesty.

FREEDOM AND THE BODY

WE HAVE ALREADY encountered one episode where Paul's lack of precision in what he said led to a misunderstanding on the part of the Corinthians, which had disastrous consequences for the community (5:9–13). It is very likely that we have a similar case here.

I Can Do Whatever I Like!

ALL PAUL'S COMMUNITIES were mixed, a few converts from Judaism but the majority from paganism. At the beginning he permitted Jews to observe the Law of Moses, while insisting that this Law did not bind Christians of pagan origin. Eventually, however, circumstances (Galatians 2:11–14) forced Paul to recognize that if the Law was accepted by any part of a Christian community it would take over. It is much easier to be a legalist, and to observe all the demands of the Law, than to be a follower of Christ called to sacrifice. The droning of lawyers makes it impossible to hear the voice from the cross. The shortsightedness engendered by tight focus on legal details rules out discernment of the needs of others.

Thus Paul came to believe very strongly that law as such, and not merely the Law of Moses, had no place in the Church. The one imperative was the example of Christ (Galatians 6:2). His radical and all-inclusive claim should not be banalized by fragmentation into precepts. The whole law was summed up in one command, "You shall love your neighbor as yourself" (Romans 13:9).

The Corinthians may not have been particularly law-abiding but, like everyone else, they liked to have the law to fall back on (6:1–8). In order to get through to them Paul found a single, striking phrase, "You are not bound by any law!" He never thought for a minute that the Corinthians would draw the obvious conclusion, "Everything is permitted! We can do what we like without any restraint!"

Paul was deeply upset. Why could they not see what this would do to the Church? Hence, belatedly, he introduces the required qualifications.

What Christians freely choose to do must be helpful to the community, and must not drag them down to the state of slavery to sin in which they had lived before their conversion.

The Importance of the Body

IF PAUL WAS indirectly responsible for the freedom slogan of the Corinthians, he cannot be blamed for their declaration of the moral irrelevance of the body. Nothing he ever said can be interpreted in this sense.

For many centuries Greek philosophers had taught that the body was the prison of the soul, which is the highest part of the human person. The physical drive toward sex and all forms of pleasure interfered with the spiritual activities of the soul. Hence the liberation of the soul through death was the greatest good.

The intellectuals at Corinth took this common view a step further. If the body is only a danger, they said, then it is unimportant and should be ignored, particularly since its activities are not restrained by any law, as far as Christians are concerned. The fact that bodily activities, like eating, come to an end at death proves that they are fundamentally nothing, totally without meaning.

Paul's retort is unusually calm, perhaps because he knew he had the winning card. The Corinthians believed in Jesus Christ who had been raised from the dead (15:3–7). But resurrection necessarily involves the body. Hence the action of God in raising Christ demonstrates the importance and significance of the body. It is the arena in which spiritual decisions become real and effective.

PRAYER

God, grant that we may use our freedom to be servants of one another.

SEX WITH A PROSTITUTE

IT IS OFTEN said that Corinth was *the* sex city of the ancient world. In fact it was no worse than any other port in the Mediterranean Sea. At one stage, in the fourth century B.C., the envy of Athens at Corinth's commercial success gave rise to a series of jibes. A "Corinthian girl" meant a prostitute. "To Corinthianize" meant to act like a pimp. But the phrases won no permanent place in the language. The first-century Roman geographer, Strabo, claimed that there were a thousand sacred prostitutes in the temple of Aphrodite, but we now know that he (or his sources) confused Corinth with another city.

Sinless Sex for Sale

STRABO WAS NOT far from the truth, however, in interpreting the proverb, "Not for everyone is the journey to Corinth," in terms of sexual promiscuity. Those who were not prepared to play should stay away from Corinth. A visit would be as pointless as a nongambler's going to Las Vegas.

Prostitutes were certainly easily available at Corinth. Some members of the Church, prior to their conversion, undoubtedly frequented them and continued to do so after baptism. They saw no reason to change their habits. As we have seen, they believed Paul to have told them that any prohibition that might have existed was no longer binding. And they themselves had come to the conclusion that no bodily action could be considered a sin. Sex, in their view, was as natural as eating, and just as neutral. To eat is neither good nor bad; similarly all other physical acts, including sexual intercourse.

True sin, the Corinthians were convinced, had to be outside the body. It could only be in the mind. Were they asked what sort of thing they considered a sin, they would have replied, "A negative spiritual act, like denying the existence of God or attributing evil to God or believing in the existence of idols."

Physical Actions Say Something

PAUL HAS ALREADY established that the human body is important in God's eyes, and has a definite place in his plan of salvation (6:12–14). Hence it cannot be ruled out of any discussion of morality. Moreover, Paul insisted, physical acts say something in and of themselves, irrespective of the intention of the one making them. A wave conveys a greeting, whatever the person might be thinking. A dissident who salutes a dictator manifests respect even though he or she may be cursing internally.

The sex act created a permanent bond. How did Paul know? The book of Genesis, which outlined God's purpose for his human creatures, told him that physical love made two people "one flesh." They were, so to speak, fused into one. The truth of this is evident in people who have been happily married for a long time. They are incomplete without each other. Sex with a prostitute, however, is by definition transitory. Permanence and stability are deliberately excluded. The act, therefore, is a lie.

Moreover, believers were members of the Body of Christ. They were united with Christ. If they were also united with a prostitute in sex, then Christ would be the third in the bed. Paul is not so crude, but this is the implication of his image of mingling the legs of Christ with those of the prostitute.

Finally, Paul capitalizes on the Corinthians' cherished belief that they possessed the Spirit. The Spirit, however, is the Spirit of God. Thus God dwells within them, making them temples of God (3:16). Their bodies, in consequence, are holy, and must be used to give glory to God, not to act out a lie and insult Christ.

PRAYER

May the knowledge that my body is a temple of the Holy Spirit express itself in acts that glorify God.

SEX IN MARRIAGE

PAUL COULD BE rigidly dogmatic on certain issues, notably, the need for believers to be followers of Christ in self-sacrificing love. When it came to working out what this meant in daily living, he not only refused to lay down any rules, but he did not believe that what was best in theory was necessarily the best in practice for any particular individual. Everyone differed in gifts, interests, stamina. What was appropriate for one might be unsuitable for another.

No Sex in Marriage

SUCH TOLERANCE HAD little impact at Corinth. There were strong personalities who believed that the spiritual paths that had led them to the heights should be imposed on all. Teaching on sex and marriage became a battleground on which no one would give way. To break the deadlock they wrote to Paul (7:1), asking for his opinion.

If some at Corinth felt that visits to a prostitute had no detrimental effect on their spiritual lives, others believed that sexual intercourse between husband and wife should be avoided. "It is good," they insisted, "that a man not touch a woman." The difference highlights the wide spectrum of views within the community, and it is easy to imagine how heated must have been the debate between those who favored total promiscuity and those who advocated the most severe asceticism.

There is nothing in Judaism or paganism that would explain why some at Corinth wanted to forbid sexual intercourse in marriage. Both considered it perfectly normal, and neither established any special relation between it and worship. We can only conclude that it is another example (cf. 5:1) of the Corinthians' preference for the bizarre in order to carry out Paul's missionary policy that Christians should be different from their neighbors in order to hold fast the word of life (Philippians 2:14–16). If only Christian married couples abstained from sex, the church would stand out as unique.

Common Sense

THE FACT THAT the Corinthians were trying to live up to Paul's ambition for them tempered his irritation with their childishness (3:1; 14:20), and he laid out his response with calm logic. The underlying principle is that God's will for believers is shown in the gifts he has given them. These gifts are pointers to the way they should live, and should not be denied. Thus those who have been given the grace of matrimony should not pretend that they have also been given the contradictory grace of celibacy. Had God willed them to be celibate, he would not have called them to marriage.

This does not mean, however, that a couple could never abstain from sexual relations. Paul would be the first to say that they are responsible for their own lives. The decision is theirs, but Paul insists that it must meet two conditions.

Obviously the abstention must be of short duration. More importantly, both parties must agree. Sex is a right inherent in marriage and it cannot be withheld unilaterally. Those who are offended by what they take to be the cold legalism of Paul's approach to the act of love ignore the fact that he treats the wife as the full equal of her husband. This was extraordinary in a society which recognized only the conjugal rights of the husband. The wife must submit; she could not demand. In Paul's eyes intercourse is a privilege and a duty for both.

Indirectly Paul is telling the Corinthians that, if they wished to be different from their neighbors in an authentically Christian sense, they should treat women as equals!

PRAYER

Lord, never let me attempt to impose a doctrinaire vision of the following of Christ on others, but make me alert to see and encourage the call reflected in their gifts.

As the Spirit Gives

PAUL BELIEVED VERY strongly that binding rules and regulations had no place in the Christian community. Goodness had to be freely chosen; it could not be compelled (Philemon 14). Occasionally, however, he orders his readers to do something. We know that this is just a slip of the tongue which should not be used to contradict his general principle, because on at least two occasions he corrects himself.

Paul appears to order the Corinthians to participate in the collection of money for the poor of Jerusalem, but immediately catches himself: "I say this not as a command" (2 Corinthians 8:8). Similarly here he has just told the Corinthians, "Do not refuse one another" (7:5), which is an order; but he continues, "I do not say this as a command" (7:6). He also intends this statement to control the interpretation of all that follows. Paul is covering himself in case he makes another slip. The Corinthians had misunderstood him several times already by taking him literally (5:9; 6:12).

A Single Man

WHEN HE WROTE this letter Paul was single. Had he chosen celibacy, postponed marriage, been divorced or widowed? The first possibility is the most unlikely. The prophetic gesture of Jeremiah—"The word of the Lord came to me: 'You shall not take a wife nor shall you have sons or daughters in this place' " (16:1–2)—was exceptional. Jews understood Genesis 1:28 as imposing an obligation to marry.

The boastful satisfaction with which Paul proclaimed his perfect observance of the Law and traditions as a Pharisee (Galatians 1:14; Philippians 3:5) is a guarantee that he had married young. The ideal age was between eighteen and twenty. A refusal to obey this commandment could not be hidden. His single state would necessarily have been a matter of public knowledge, and he would have been condemned as a failure, particularly in the competitive world of the Pharisees.

Thus when he wrote 1 Corinthians Paul was probably either divorced or widowed. A case can be made for both options, but I prefer to think of him as widowed. The accidental death of his wife and children would have generated an anger that explains his persecution of Christians. According to the Acts of the Apostles, all the early persecutions of the Church were unleashed by the Sadducees. No Pharisees were involved, with the exception of Paul. Why he was different calls for some explanation.

The Advantages of Celibacy

PAUL NEVER REMARRIED. Perhaps he found no one to replace his first love. It is more likely, however, that he judged that his life had no place for a wife. He was a wandering missionary without a home who had great difficulty paying his way. He had nothing to offer a woman, and she would have been a distraction. Being alone he was able to give himself totally to his ministry.

Inevitably, therefore, Paul thought celibacy the best state for all Christians, who were by definition missionaries. To spread the gospel was intrinsic to their vocation. The freer they were to respond to the needs of others, the better.

But this was only theory, and Paul had no intention of imposing what he knew to be best for him on others. If they wanted to get married, they were perfectly free to do so. In fact they would probably be better Christians if they did marry. Those distracted by unfulfilled passionate desires cannot be attentive to others, and are likely to fall into illicit relationships. Paul's pragmatism is seldom so evident.

PRAYER

God grant that I may have the courage to correct myself when necessary, and to choose a lifestyle that expresses my God-given gifts.

A DIVORCE DENIED

IN JEWISH LAW a man could divorce his wife, but she could not divorce him. She could only petition the court to bring pressure on her husband to set her free. If the husband refused to budge, the court could not set him aside and give the divorce itself.

Not surprisingly, therefore, Jesus' prohibition of divorce mentions only the husband: "Everyone who divorces his wife and marries another commits adultery, and he who marries a woman divorced from her husband commits adultery" (Luke 16:18). This decision envisages two different cases. A married man may go through a divorce procedure but in the eyes of God he is not free to contract a second marriage. A single man cannot marry a divorced woman because as far as God is concerned she is still married.

Why Does Paul Mention Divorce?

IF PAUL SIMPLY intended to proclaim the teaching of Jesus on the indissolubility of marriage he went about it in a very curious way. He introduces it merely as an afterthought. In effect he says, "Here is my opinion regarding those already married—oops! I have just realized that Jesus agrees with me!" Moreover, he does not focus exclusively on the husband. In fact the wife is mentioned first, and her remarriage (but not his!) is explicitly excluded. These points suggest that something much more complicated is going on here than a simple repetition of Jesus' teaching.

The Angry Wife

A CURIOUS SITUATION had developed in Corinth. A husband had been impressed by the arguments of the ascetics who asserted that married Christians would be better off spiritually if they did not have sexual intercourse, and informed his wife that they would no longer have sex. The unfortunate woman had never heard anything more stupid, and forcefully and frequently expressed her feelings on being excluded from the marriage bed. The husband did not have a moment's peace. To get her out of his hair he decided to divorce his wife.

This was the state of affairs when Paul heard what was going on. He used the prohibition of Jesus to reinforce his own opinion that the wife should not permit herself to be divorced. She should refuse to accept the divorce document. If it were forced upon her, however, she should resist the temptation to rush into another marriage.

A Eunuch for the Kingdom of Heaven

PAUL ACTED AS he did not because he felt bound by the decision of Jesus (as we shall see in the next section), but because he thought the reasons for this particular divorce foolish. In 7:1–5 he had made it perfectly clear that sex in marriage was a good thing. His arguments when read out in public had a chance of influencing the husband. Moreover the sexual urge is much stronger than idealistic theories. Time should bring the husband to his senses.

In this case he would want to apologize to his wife and to resume the marriage. But what if she had remarried? She could never forgive her ex-husband fully by going back to the point in their lives before his silly mistake. This is why Paul asked her to remain single. She should "make herself a eunuch for the sake of the kingdom of heaven" (Matthew 19:12), waiting patiently for the man she had married to change his mind.

While admitting that she was the injured party, Paul asked her for a generous love that would keep the door of complete forgiveness open for as long as it took. Christ does not love us because we are good. His love makes us good, and the wife should channel that love to her ex-husband.

PRAYER
God, enable me to truly love my enemies.

STRESS IN MARRIAGE

THE CORINTHIANS UNDERSTOOD at least the principle behind Paul's teaching on freedom. They recognized that the force of the good example of other members in a community of love protected them from the bad example of society. Since they did not live with sinners, they were freed from the power of sin.

Not surprisingly, therefore, some at Corinth raised objections to marriages in which only one partner had become a Christian. Such marriages, they insisted, should be dissolved, because the nonbelieving partner lived by the standards of the world. The proximity of the pagan weakened the protection from sin that the community offered. He or she lived by different ideals.

Paul did not believe that one decision would cover all cases. The circumstances of each situation made a difference. Hence he says both Yes and No.

An Opportunity for Conversion

IN THE CASE where the nonbelieving partner wanted to preserve the marriage, Paul says there should be no divorce. The community should capitalize on the goodwill shown by the pagan in accepting the conversion of, and in wanting to live with, the believer. It was a golden opportunity to persuade the pagan to become a Christian, as Peter had seen: "Wives, be submissive to your husbands, so that some, though they do not obey the word, may be won without a word by the behavior of their wives" (1 Peter 3:1).

Contrary to what the Corinthians might have expected, Paul does not say that the believer is defiled by the unconverted spouse, but that the pagan is sanctified by the Christian. Nowhere else does Paul attribute "holiness" to a nonbeliever. He reserves the term "saint" for Christians (1:2). But the behavior of the pagan here justifies his language. The pagan is affirming the divine order that marriage makes two people "one flesh"

(6:16) and, by resisting the pressure to break up the marriage, he is obeying Jesus' prohibition of divorce (7:11). In other words, the nonbeliever is doing just what believers should do. He is acting as if he were a "holy" Christian.

Realizing that the Corinthians might be disturbed by his terminology, Paul points out that they themselves used the same language in other circumstances. Even though their children were unbaptized, and technically unbelievers, no one at Corinth thought of the children as "little pagans"—Jews considered pagans "unclean"—but as "holy." The children had been born into freedom. They were never under the power of sin. They imitated the Christian behavior of their parents.

A Justifiable Divorce

IN THE CASE where the unbelieving partner did not wish to continue the marriage, Paul agrees that there should be a divorce. The pagan's attitude made conversion a very remote possibility. He or she was actively hostile to Christianity, and blamed the Church for transforming a harmonious marriage into an exhausting hell of bitter arguments. No one so tormented could live a Christian life, and Paul thought it reasonable that the marriage should be broken up.

Paul found Jesus' prohibition of divorce useful in the case of the antisex husband (7:10–11), but he did not believe that any precept was binding (Philemon 14). Here he invokes the principle "God has called us to peace" (7:15) to underline that it cannot be his will to continue a situation where there was no peace.

Paul says nothing about remarriage, because in his world the act of divorce was the authorization to contract another marriage. According to Jewish law, "The essential formula in the bill of divorce is, 'Behold, you are free to marry any man.' Rabbi Judah says: 'Let this be from me your writ of divorce and letter of dismissal and deed of liberation, that you may marry whatever man you wish'" (m. Gittin 9:3).

PRAYER
God, grant that my deeds may match my intentions.

CHANGES IN SOCIAL STATUS

THE PROBLEMS WITH which Paul has dealt earlier in this chapter reveal the belief of at least some of the Corinthians that one's relationship with God would be improved by a change in social status. The married would be better off if they were celibate. Those in mixed marriages would gain by becoming single again.

A Foolish Principle

IN EACH INSTANCE Paul's answer was essentially "Yes, but," because circumstances alter cases. Now he formulates a general principle to cover all such situations: "Each one should retain the place in life that the Lord assigned to him, and to which God has called him" (7:16; cf. 7:20).

At this point one begins to have a certain sympathy for the Corinthians because, when taken literally, this is nonsense. It means that the poverty of the poor is willed by God; hence they should not try to improve their lot! Equally the wealth of the rich is an element in God's plan for them; in consequence they should never give it all away even for Christ's sake! Also, those who had the misfortune to become Christians when single could never marry.

Obviously Paul has put his foot in it once again and made the atmosphere in the community worse. His friends cursed him for using words that could not be trusted. As they struggled to work out what he really meant, they had to put up with the triumphant "I told you so!" of his enemies. Smiling happily, the intellectuals insisted on the literal meaning. It made Paul look the fool they had always said he was.

Two Examples

AS USUAL, WHAT Paul intended to say is perfectly sensible: A person's relationship with God is conditioned exclusively by the practice of faith, hope, and charity (1 Thessalonians 1:3), and these have absolutely nothing to do with social status. A slave can love as truly as the greatest king.

Moreover, the call of God came to individuals in the most diverse settings. He summoned the wealthy and the poor indiscriminately. In Christian terms, therefore, one's place in society is irrelevant. Thus it is futile to try to change it.

The first example Paul uses is very effective. Some male members of the community were Jews when they became Christians, others were Gentiles. One group was circumcised, the other was not. Would it make the slightest difference to their Christianity if the Gentiles underwent a very painful operation to remove the foreskin, or if the Jews suffered an equally painful operation to put it back? Obviously not. Loving God and one's neighbor are all that matter.

The second example is much less clear. The word of God came equally to slave and free, so it was irrelevant which a person was. Thus from one point of view it was futile for a slave to want to be free, though from another it was tremendously important. Freed slaves became legal persons instead of pieces of property. They had to be treated as human beings, whereas before they were socially dead. Inevitably all slaves desired to be free.

Paul was not opposed to this desire. He knew that virtually all slaves were freed in their thirties, and he had no objection to this change over which the slave had no control. What he did not want was agitation that would rock the social and economic framework of his world. Slaves made up roughly 30 percent of the population of any city, and an uprising would cause immense suffering. To save the lives of others, therefore, slaves should be patient. Christianity gave them their human rights. There was no longer any distinction between slave and free in the Church (Galatians 3:28). Eventually society would catch up.

PRAYER
God, grant that I may express my ideas accurately, and be patient with those who are confused and obscure.

ENGAGED COUPLES

THOSE AT CORINTH who had persuaded the husband to deny his wife her conjugal rights (7:1–11) had not restricted their interference in the lives of others to married couples. Their refusal to see sexual intercourse as good and natural led them to bring pressure to bear on engaged couples, telling them that they should not follow through on their mutual promise to marry. They would be better off spiritually, the ascetics insisted, if they gave up all thoughts of a relationship that was fundamentally sexual.

Life in Limbo

ALTHOUGH A CITY in Greece, Corinth was a Roman colony. However, if the legislation was Roman, for Greek families traditional customs had the force of law. In Roman law an engagement was informal and not binding. The marriage contract was signed when the couple took up residence together.

Greek law demanded a binding, witnessed engagement agreement, which in effect became the marriage contract when the bride went to live in the groom's house. The favored month for weddings was January, when work was slack in all fields.

In Greece men married about the age of thirty. Women were usually married by the time they reached sixteen. In the situation that Paul has in view here, one can be fairly certain that it was the young woman who listened to the ascetics. Idealistic and a virgin, she would have been fair game for their challenges to spiritual perfection. Her fiancé might have been persuaded by her charms momentarily, but second thoughts would not have been long delayed. Should they, could they, repudiate the engagement agreement? The engaged couple lived in a state of limbo, unsure whether to go backward or forward.

On the Horns of a Dilemma

ALL THE SUGGESTIONS that Paul had offered hitherto would lead one to conclude that in this instance he would side with the ascetics. He had opposed voluntary change of social status (7:12–24). He had also expressed a preference for celibacy (7:7). Unless Paul was to be totally inconsistent he had to agree with those who wanted young people to remain single.

Once again Paul found himself with a problem. He could not go back on what he had said, but the reasoning of the ascetics contradicted his principle that a person's lifestyle should be decided by the gifts God had given that person (7:7), not by any theoretical decision as to what is best in principle.

Paul's problem was to find a way to affirm the position of the ascetics, which in this instance he instinctively favored, while denying their argument that sex was bad. He did so by enlarging the problem and putting it in an entirely pragmatic framework. What was most sensible in practice should take priority over what was best in theory.

As he will explain in the next section (7:29–32), Paul was convinced that very shortly the world in which they all lived was going to go through a period of catastrophic turmoil. It was not the time to mess around. The boat should not be rocked just as it is heading for the rapids. It was not the moment to make major changes in one's life.

Thus to start divorce proceedings or to enter into an engagement agreement right now would be unwise. It would be a major distraction at a time when believers needed all their wits about them. Paul's sense of urgency makes him speak in commands: "Do not separate," "Do not marry"; but typically (7:6) he immediately says that these orders are not binding. Those who really want to get married should go ahead. Their decision is in no way wrong. Paul's genuine pastoral concern for each individual makes him as different from the dogmatic ascetics as chalk from cheese.

PRAYER

God, let me never interfere in the lives of others in the belief that I know what is best for them. Rather help me to aid them in the discernment of their own gifts.

THE TIME IS SHORT

PAUL HAD SPENT his formative years at a pagan university in Tarsus, but he was a Jew; and after he came to Jerusalem at about the age of twenty, he spent over ten years as a Pharisee there prior to his conversion. With enthusiastic commitment he thoroughly steeped himself in the theological outlook of his people.

The Last Day

JEWS BELIEVED THAT events in history revealed the working out of God's purpose for humanity. Nothing was beyond the reach of his will. If God permitted evil to exist, it was because he intended to punish it at an appropriate moment. The wicked, however, were so intermingled with good people that in the popular mind it seemed inevitable that the punishment of the wicked would have unfortunate consequences for the good.

If, for example, God used an earthquake to wipe out the wicked in Jerusalem, would not the houses of the good fall down as well? Not surprisingly there was consistent interest among Jews as to when this terrible moment would come. To use the same example, those who were forewarned would not be in their houses when the earthquake struck.

It was generally believed that prophecies contained clues to the date of the last day. Some resorted to complicated calculations. Others watched for the signs of the times. One key sign, whose importance all Jews recognized, would be the appearance of the Messiah, the final agent of God in history.

Hang Loose

FOR PAUL THE Messiah had already come in the person of Jesus of Nazareth. His title "the Christ" is simply the Greek translation of the Hebrew "Messiah." In consequence, Paul believed that the last day was just around the corner. There was very little time left. To plan far ahead was pointless.

From Paul's perspective, the Corinthians should have worked this out for themselves. Perhaps the few Jewish converts did, but the pagan members of the Church lacked the background to make such a deduction. The Greco-Roman world dreamed vaguely of a golden age in which the greatness of the past would be renewed in an even more perfect future. But it was not an idea that excited much interest. It never attracted the intense expectation that colored Jewish speculation. The vast majority of individuals never thought of the world coming to an end.

For Paul this was dangerous complacency, a barrier that blocked the Corinthians from dealing with reality. In order to break through it he used language so striking that the eyes of his readers must have opened wide with astonishment. Husbands should pretend that they were single. The sorrowful should pretend to be happy. The happy should pretend to be sorrowful. Those who bought should pretend that their shopping bags were empty. Those who sold should pretend that they had no customers.

Here we catch a glimpse of the quality of Paul's education. This is rhetorical skill of the highest order. The vivid phrases cannot be taken literally, but they have to be taken seriously. Of course, he expected husbands to continue loving their wives. He knew perfectly well that mourners would still weep, just as the joyful would still laugh. But Paul wanted to shock people into the realization that these were all transitory activities. One should not get absorbed in them. Neither pleasure nor pain are permanent, and should not determine the way we direct our lives.

What was true on the individual level was also true on the institutional level. Social and economic systems were no more permanent than human emotions. They were already being eaten away by a relentless corrosion that could not be reversed. Any serious investment in such systems was not only pointless but dangerous. One's attention should be focused on the things that really matter.

PRAYER

God, let me be deeply involved with the improvement of my world while knowing that it will not last.

FREEDOM FROM ANXIETY

"I WANT YOU to be free from care." If I had to select one phrase from all of Paul's letters to sum up what he hoped to achieve by his ministry within each of his communities, this would be my choice. Once "care" is understood as "anxious concern," its relevance to our situation is as obvious as it was to Paul's readers.

Care and Anxiety

ACCORDING TO A Greek creation story recorded in the second century A.D., Care one day found some clay which she molded into a human figure. As she gazed at what she had made, Jupiter appeared, and at her request he gave it spirit. Care wanted it to bear her name, but Jupiter refused and insisted that it bear his. Earth complicated the situation further by claiming that it should rather bear her name, since she had given a piece of her body. Saturn was brought in to adjudicate. He decreed that at its death Jupiter should take the spirit and Earth the body, but while the human figure lived it belonged to Care (Macquarrie, *Existentialist Theology,* 114).

The point of this story is that humanity was created for a life of care, a life poisoned by a persistent anxiety that something had gone seriously wrong. Paul did not believe that this was the purpose of human existence, but as a man of his century he knew that this was how people really felt. His contemporaries might walk with their heads held high, but inwardly they cowered before an impending catastrophe that they could neither identify nor anticipate. The prevailing state of mind can be illustrated in our century by a couple whose holiday is ruined by the unspoken fear that a tap may have been left running or a window open at home. Such "anxious concern" for their possessions takes all the joy out of days that were meant to be carefree.

Freedom from Care

PAGANS BELIEVED THAT "care" was integral to being human. Life was unthinkable without it. It could never be avoided. Jesus, however, had taught Paul that "care" could be set aside provided that one had the right priorities. "Do not be anxious, saying, 'What shall we eat?' or 'What shall we drink?' or 'What shall we wear?' For the Gentiles seek all these things, and your heavenly Father knows that you need them all. But seek first his kingdom and his righteousness, and all these things will be yours as well" (Matthew 6:31–32). How? God's kingdom on earth is a community of love in which each is concerned, not for him- or herself, but for the needs of the other.

The situations on which Paul focuses might give the impression that to be single is intrinsically better than to be married. The married couple, he says, is totally absorbed in how to please each other, whereas "the unmarried man/woman/virgin is anxious about the affairs of the Lord, how to please the Lord." Neither statement is true. Many married people are dedicated to the service of others, and many single people are selfish. If the married are divided because they love both each other and God, are not singles divided by the need to love both their neighbor and God?

So what is Paul getting at? He is critical of the "anxiety" displayed by both married and single. "Anxious concern" is out of place for Christians, no matter what their state in life. The married may be distracted by mundane matters, as the ascetics no doubt pointed out, but they ignored the possibility that the effort of the unmarried to please God may be a fawning servility characterized by worry about success.

Our state in life is irrelevant to our relationship to God, which depends exclusively on a generous love that is the antidote to care.

PRAYER
Lord, make me carefree. Smother my doubts and worries with the love
you channel to me through others.

FOLLOW YOUR HEART

THE RATHER DIFFIDENT, almost plaintive conclusion to the previous section—"I say this for your own benefit, not to lay any restraint upon you"—shows that Paul has cooled down considerably since his savage outbursts in the early part of this letter. This was probably due to two factors.

First, he was forced to realize that his somewhat simplistic approach—"Work out yourselves what being a Christian involves!"—had not taken into account the fact that there could be honest differences of opinion between himself and the Corinthians and among the Corinthians themselves. Second, Paul accepted that he must carry some of the responsibility for misunderstandings. Thinking of Christ he had stressed self-sacrifice, but the ascetics interpreted it differently. What could be a greater sacrifice than giving up sex?

Marriage is Not a Sin

THE INSIDIOUS PLAUSIBILITY of this view decided Paul to return to the issue of engaged couples. He does not really say anything different from what he has written earlier (7:25–28), but he does so in a way so convoluted that it has given rise to a great deal of debate.

The problem, which has bedeviled translators, can be put as a question: Why would an engaged person feel that marriage was imperative? The answer, of course, is: a very strong, almost uncontrollable, sex drive. Paul does not make it clear whether he is thinking of the man or the woman. In either case, however, whether the man beseeches the woman to marry, or she him, Paul is definite that they should wed. Unsatisfied sexual urges can only turn the person inward in agony, the antithesis of the way believers should live. Christians must ever be attentive to the needs of others.

Paul, however, knew that some people have either a weak sex drive or a very strong will. In this case it would be relatively easy to forgo marriage without hindering their Christian life, and Paul applauds those who opt for celibacy. These "do better," not because celibacy is intrinsically superior, but because it is normal to rate higher those who keep a commitment than those who break a promise, no matter how valid the justification might be. In neither case is there any question of sin.

Remarriage

HAVING DEALT WITH those who had chosen celibacy and subsequently found that they could or could not keep their promise, Paul then turned to those whose spouses had died. Through no choice of their own the survivors found themselves in the single state that Paul had repeatedly said was preferable. Could they remarry?

The question arises logically out of the preceding discussion, but there may be more to it than that. There were Essenes, the Jewish group that produced the Dead Sea Scrolls, in the hinterland of Ephesus, the city in which Paul wrote this letter. They permitted only one marriage because in their view the mutual commitment of husband and wife was not broken by death. The two were one flesh for eternity. This vision commands respect for its idealism, but Paul remains faithful to his pragmatic principle that people's gifts are known from their lifestyles (7:7). Manifestly anyone who had been married was not destined for celibacy. The survivor, therefore, was free to remarry. Paul, however, once again cannot refrain from reiterating that celibacy is the better practical decision as the present world draws to a close.

Paul's focus on the woman may reflect the fact that even in antiquity women lived longer than men. What he says about a widow, of course, applies equally to a widower.

The right of remarriage is limited by one condition. The new partner must be a Christian. This is eminent common sense. Remarriage would certainly complicate one's life. Why make it impossibly difficult by selecting a pagan partner with radically different views on fundamental issues?

INTENSIVE DIALOGUE

THE VOICES OF members of the Corinthian Church that we had to struggle to discern in the last chapter here speak out loud and clear. It is difficult to be sure why Paul does not always permit us to hear the voices of those to whom he is replying. Perhaps in some cases the expression of the Corinthians' ideas was diffuse and long-winded. Clear, brief phrases, as in 6:12–20 and here, were more suited to citation. Once again, therefore, in order to grasp the dialogue structure of this important chapter, it is imperative to set out the text as if it were a script for a play. It is also necessary to correct the standard translations at crucial points.

The Dialogue

PAUL: Now, concerning food offered to idols!

CORINTHIANS: All of us possess knowledge!

PAUL: Knowledge puffs up, but love builds up. If anyone thinks that he has acquired full knowledge, he does not yet know as he ought to know. But if one loves, one truly knows.

CORINTHIANS: An idol has no real existence. There is only one God.

PAUL: Although there may be so-called gods in heaven or on earth—as in fact there are many "gods" and many "lords"—yet for us there is "one God, the Father, from whom come all things and to whom we go, and one Lord, Jesus Christ, through whom come all things and through whom we go."

It is not everyone, however, who has this knowledge. Since some have become so accustomed to idols until now, they still think of the food they eat as food offered to an idol; and their conscience, being weak, is defiled.

CORINTHIANS: Food will not bring us before the judgment seat of God. We are neither better off if we do not eat, nor worse off if we do eat.

PAUL: Take care lest this liberty of yours become a stumbling block to the weak. For if others see you, who possess knowledge, eating in the temple of an idol, might not the conscience of a weak person be "edified" to eat food offered to idols? And so by your knowledge, this weak person is destroyed, the fellow-believer for whom Christ died. Thus, sinning against your fellow-believers, and wounding their weak conscience, you sin against Christ.

Therefore, if food is a cause of one of my fellow-believers' falling, I will never eat idol meat, lest I cause a fellow-believer to fall.

The Problem

THE WAY IN which Paul introduces the problem shows it to have been raised by the Corinthians in their letter (7:1). The importance given to fish in the gospels (Mark 6:38; Matthew 7:10; 13:47–48; Luke 24:42) underlines that it was the main source of protein in the ancient world. Some 200 different types of edible fish were available in the eastern Mediterranean. Meat was too expensive for the vast majority. It became available cheaply only on the occasion of great Jewish or pagan feasts when many sacrifices were offered. The priests received far too much for themselves and their families to eat, and sold the surplus to supplement their income. Volume and the lack of refrigeration created a buyers' market, and those who lived on pickled or salted fish jumped at the chance of eating fresh meat. It was the treat of the year.

For Jews in Jerusalem there was no problem. The sacrifices had been offered to the one true God. It was a different matter in the cities in which Paul worked. All the sacrifices that provided cheap meat were offered to idols. Inevitably, scrupulous members of the Church wondered if this put such meat out of bounds for Christians. They were opposed by other believers who put forward arguments to justify their right to eat idol meat. It is with the latter that Paul is in dialogue.

PRAYER

God, grant that I may reply with gentleness and honesty to those who disagree with me.

Love Is True Knowledge

THE FIRST STEP in the argument of those at Corinth who believed that they were fully justified in enjoying the cheap meat that became available on the occasion of great public feasts was "All of us possess knowledge!" This banal statement of the obvious provoked a surprisingly sharp response from Paul.

Knowing and Knowledge

PAUL WOULD HAVE reacted differently had the Corinthians said "We know." It would have been pointless to dispute the manifest truth that every human being knows something. But what they said was literally "We have knowledge." "Knowledge" is a commodity that is possessed. The hint that we have to deal with a technical term with a specialized meaning is confirmed by the fact that at the very beginning of this letter Paul had complimented the Corinthians on their "knowledge" (1:5). We noted there that this was to damn with faint praise. Faith, hope, and charity were the virtues that Paul really desired in his converts (1 Thessalonians 1:3). Yet 12:8 and 13:2 list "knowledge" as a gift of the Holy Spirit. As a divine charism it must be good. How then can Paul permit himself to be critical of it? Obviously he does not criticize the gift in itself, but the use that some at Corinth made of it.

In the first four chapters of this letter Paul came down heavily on the pretensions of the intellectuals who caused the divisions within the Church at Corinth. The wisdom of knowledge was everything to them. They flattered themselves that their speculation on the mysteries of God demonstrated their superiority over others. They made religion a matter of the mind, and preened themselves on the perfection achieved by knowledge. Paul, as we have seen, used savage sarcasm to prick the bubble of their complacency (4:8). Here he recalls all that by the dismissive phrase "knowledge puffs up." Those who prided themselves on their "knowledge" did not know the simple truth that "love" is the source of authentic knowledge.

A Textual Problem

THE TEXT OF 8:2–3 that appears in all Bibles reads in the most literal translation, "If anyone imagines that he has achieved knowledge [of something], he does not yet know as he ought to know. But if one loves [God], one knows/is known [by him]." The first sentence is nonsense. Those who have achieved the knowledge that $2 + 2 = 4$ know exactly as they ought to know. The second sentence does not fit the argument, which is concerned not with love of God, but with love of neighbor.

These observations force us to recognize that the text is corrupted. Errors have crept in through careless copying. The bracketed words, which cause all the trouble, are lacking in the oldest version of this text. If we omit these words a lucid and appropriate text, which is authentically Pauline, emerges: "If anyone imagines that he has achieved knowledge, he does not yet know as he ought to know. But if one loves, one knows."

Love and Knowledge

PAUL'S CRITICISM OF the intellectuals at Corinth was that their "knowledge" made them turn inward on themselves. Their intense focus on what they knew about God and his plan of salvation made them oblivious to the needs of others. As so often, those "in the know" erected barriers to keep out those who were not so favored. As far as Paul was concerned, this could not be Christian.

Genuine knowledge in the Christian sense must be born of love, because its goal is not an idea or a synthesis but a profound insight into what one's neighbor wants. Elsewhere Paul says, "It is my prayer that your love may abound more and more with knowledge and all discernment" (Philippians 1:9). The lover detects the needs of the beloved even before the latter is aware of them.

PRAYER
Lord, let me not impose dogma, but discern need.

REALITY TEST

THE CHRISTIANS AT Corinth who ate meat that had been sacrificed to idols were wrong, but not because their moral reasoning was flawed. Their argument was consistent and flowed from an indisputable premise. Their mistake was to think that their logic reflected reality. In fact they imposed a false simplicity on a very complex situation. They took a shortcut which did not pay off.

The Simple Argument

LIKE ALL THE great cities of antiquity Corinth contained a multitude of places of worship. A very early guidebook to the city written by Pausanias about A.D. 170 mentions temples of Apollo, Athena, Aphrodite, Asclepius, Poseidon, Demeter, Kore, and Isis. And just in case any god might feel left out there was a temple dedicated to "all the gods."

To this rampant polytheism Paul opposed a firm monotheism, which was obligatory for all his converts (1 Thessalonians 1:9). By the first century the practical monotheism of early Israel, represented by exclusive worship of one God, had long given way to the absolute monotheism which affirmed that only one God existed (Deuteronomy 6:4; Isaiah 40:25). The other side of this coin was the denial of any reality to idols. The prophet Isaiah said of false gods, "You are less than nothingness and what you do is less than nothing" (41:24).

The Corinthians had learned this lesson well, and drew the proper conclusion from it. If idols were only figments of the imagination, then the meat that was offered to them was not changed in any way. It was as if the meat had been put into an empty room for a brief period. The beliefs of those who made the sacrifices had no impact on the meat. In other words, nothing had happened that would put the meat out of bounds for Christians. Hence, all were free to eat idol meat.

The Complex Reality

PAUL COULD NOT object to the logic of this line of argument. Nonetheless he disagreed with the conclusion. This appears inconsistent on his part only until it is recognized that the purely intellectual approach to the problem was too narrow to accommodate the complexity of reality.

The Corinthians had failed to take into account the frailty of human nature and the fact that some idol worshipers were Christians. Many converts, who had in principle espoused monotheism, in fact continued to believe in the power of idols. What this means in practice Paul will develop in the next section. At this point it is more important for his response to remind the Corinthians of who they were.

They had reasoned as if Christ did not exist, as if they were not Christians. Their entire focus was on the existence of one God, but they had ignored what that God had done and how he had done it. Paul could simply have told them that they owed everything to Christ, and that his example must influence every thought and action. On this occasion, however, he chose a much more dramatic approach. He quotes (8:6) the acclamation with which the Corinthians expressed their wonder at the experience of divine power which raised them from death to life in baptism. The effect was to bring them back in spirit to the moment that had changed their lives.

There are different renderings of 8:6 because the Greek contains no verbs. They have to be supplied by the translator, and different judgments are made. "From" and "to," however, clearly imply motion and weigh the balance in favor of supplying the verbs "come" and "go" rather than the static verbs "are" and "exist." The one God had initiated the process of salvation, but Christ was the effective agent. It is he "through whom all things come," and through whom we return to the Father. In consequence, he must be the central factor in all moral decisions. No believer can follow the example of the Corinthians and pretend that Christ does not exist.

PRAYER

Lord, grant me the insight to appreciate the complexity of life, and the love to live it as Christ did.

RIGHT BECOMES WRONG

IF A COURSE of action is right, is that sufficient reason for doing it? Most would answer in the affirmative. Paul says No! The intrinsic goodness of an act cannot alone authorize it. The impact of the act on others must be taken into account. The question a Christian must ask is not "Is this right or wrong?" but rather "Does this help or hinder others?" Believers may have to forgo an act that is perfectly acceptable in itself because it causes pain to another.

Reality Versus Theory

THOSE WHO ATE idol meat at Corinth did so with a clear conscience. Such meat had been offered to a nothing because there was only one God, the Father of Jesus Christ. The logic was impeccable. A certain smug satisfaction with a neat job well done is understandable. There were no loose ends. The issue was black and white.

For others in the community, things were not that simple. In accepting baptism they had committed themselves to the belief that idols did not really exist. It was the inescapable inference from monotheism. Such logic, however, ran into opposition from instinct, as it so often does. For example, statistics show that it is safer to fly than to drive. Yet many people are much more nervous in planes than in cars, because the danger of heights and the fear of falling are deeply rooted in their subconscious.

Similarly, at Corinth, some members of the Church could not fully shake the conviction of a lifetime that the pagan gods exercised real influence on their lives. Belief in the power of such gods was woven into the fabric of their personalities. It would be some time before the fabric could be unpicked and rewoven without the threads of old beliefs. Their heads made them monotheists, but they were ruled by their hearts. They felt that to eat meat offered to idols, or to participate in a temple meal, would bring them back into the orbit of powers that they had offended by denying their existence. Thus they concluded that eating idol meat was wrong, and should be avoided.

A Counterargument

THOSE WHO HAD no such scruples countered that they were in no danger of incurring God's wrath. And they offered a concrete test. Is it likely that God would give spiritual gifts to those who displeased him? On the contrary, he would rather withdraw them. Yet the spiritual gifts of those who ate idol meat had not diminished, and the gifts of those who abstained had not increased. Eating meat offered to idols, therefore, was morally neutral. God was neither for nor against it.

This argument, of course, did not deal with the irrational fears of the weak at Corinth. It was aimed at their heads, but the problem was their hearts. Moreover, for Paul it was another example of the Corinthians' tendency to set Christ aside. They did not repudiate him explicitly, but reduced him to insignificance by referring everything to God. They made the will of God, rather than the following of Christ, their criterion because the former is obscure, whereas the latter is clear. The will of God can be invoked to justify practically anything. The following of Christ summons us only to self-sacrifice.

The True Criterion of Morality

PAUL DID NOT deny that the idol-meat eaters were theoretically correct. They had "right" on their side. Nonetheless, he insists, it was not good for them to act as they did. They had sailed ahead as if they were alone in the world. They had forgotten that they were Christians. They had ignored the fact that they were members of a community. They had abrogated their responsibility for weaker, less clearsighted believers. Had they loved their neighbors, they would have made sure that they did not make life more difficult, if not impossible, for those whom conscience forced to take a different position. If they were to live *as Christians*, love made it imperative that the idol meat-eaters surrender their "right."

PRAYER
Grant, O Lord, that love of my neighbor may be the wellspring of my moral decisions.

EATING IN A PAGAN TEMPLE

CHRISTIANS IN CORINTH were in dispute as to whether it was legitimate to eat meat that had been sacrificed to idols. Some answered Yes, on intellectual grounds. These, for convenience, we can call the Strong. Others responded No, on emotional grounds. These we can call the Weak. For Paul the former were right, and the latter were wrong. Yet at the same time he insisted that the Strong should not eat idol meat, out of love for the Weak. Nothing was good in itself. An act was good if it improved the lot of others, and bad if it put obstacles in their way.

Why did Paul restrain the Strong, when apparently it would have been sufficient to persuade the two groups to agree to differ politely? He must have been told, or else had the imagination to envisage, the sort of pressure the Strong could bring to bear inadvertently on the Weak.

The Temple of Asclepius

A NUMBER OF pagan temples at Corinth offered facilities for dining. The two best preserved are the temple of Demeter and Kore on the slopes of Acrocorinth, and the temple of Asclepius just inside the great wall that bordered the city on the north. The latter admirably met the rule that healing temples should be located where there was clean air and pure water. It sat above the spring of Lerna, and got the clean air from the Gulf of Corinth before it was polluted on passing over the city. It was a pleasant and relaxing spot which attracted not only the sick but those in search of relief from the heat and noise of the city.

On a lower level a covered gallery ran around the four sides of a square courtyard. On one side three identical dining rooms opened onto the courtyard. The walls of each were lined with eleven stone couches on which the diners reclined. The food was cooked on a fireplace in the center. Seven small tables completed the arrangement. One of these dining rooms would have been a perfect place to give thanks on a joyful occasion, a birth, a coming of age, a marriage, or a successful business deal.

The Dilemma of the Weak

IN ORDER TO appreciate the sort of pressure the Strong could inadvertently bring to bear on the Weak, let us imagine that one of the latter is taking a peaceful stroll in the courtyard of the temple. All of a sudden he hears a voice from one of the dining rooms: "Come and join us!" He turns to see a group, among whom are one or two of the Strong, reclining on the couches. His employer or someone else whom he cannot afford to offend are of the party.

He is revolted by the idea of eating idol meat, but what can he offer as an excuse? The presence of the Strong makes it impossible to decline on the grounds that his new faith would not permit it. Anything less would be an insult to powerful individuals. Paul saw that, in such circumstances, the weak person would give in and participate in the feast, even though he was being forced to act against his conscience. Internally, however, he was being torn apart.

For Paul, to subject a fellow believer to such a psychological death could not be an act of love. It was destructive of the Church, and thus a sin against "Christ," which in this context can only mean the community (6:15; 12:12).

In all this Paul never tells the Strong what to do. He cannot impose a moral decision. The choice must be theirs in freedom. All he can do is to spell out the real situation so clearly that they can draw the proper conclusions themselves, and to offer the example of his own abstention from idol meat.

PRAYER
God, grant that no act of mine may provoke others to act against their consciences.

RECOGNIZING GRACE

LIKE MANY OF our contemporaries, the Strong at Corinth believed that the successful assertion of one's rights was the proof of freedom. Paul, on the contrary, maintained that renunciation was a higher use of freedom. To have a right and not to claim it manifested a confidence and authority that those who insisted on their rights lacked. His renunciation of his right to eat idol meat showed him to be freer in spirit than the Strong. He did not feel their need to be assertive.

Paul Not an Apostle

FOOD WAS NOT the only sphere in which Paul practiced renunciation. He also refused to use his right to be financed. His reason for so doing will be made clear later (9:15–18), but he raises the issue here because this self-imposed restriction had been misinterpreted at Corinth.

The fact that the Corinthians knew that Church leaders elsewhere did not have to support themselves means that they had contact with other communities. Perhaps Apollos informed them of the practice in Alexandria (Acts 18:24–25) as justification for his own claim for support. Business contacts—Corinth was an important commercial center—were another possible avenue of information. In any case, Paul's opponents interpreted his failure to use his right to support as evidence that he did not have that right. "If he were a true apostle," they argued, "he would demand that we support him financially as all other apostles do. Since he does not, we must assume that he is not a genuine apostle. He should be rejected as a faker."

Only this accusation, which cuts at the root of Paul's ministry, explains the deluge of rhetorical questions with which Paul passionately defends himself. The confident use of a delicate technique betrays his first-class education.

Seeing Jesus the Lord

THE RHETORICAL QUESTION "Have I not seen Jesus the Lord?" expects the answer Yes (as do all the others). This graphic language, which highlights the subjective activity of those privileged to encounter the Risen Christ, was an inevitable development from the original expression of the same experience: "Last of all he appeared also to me" (15:8). Paul identifies his experience on the road to Damascus as a post-resurrection appearance of Jesus.

All the earliest accounts of the Easter appearances give the initiative to Jesus, who breaks into human consciousness. The way these stories are told exclude the possibility that the disciples imagined what they wanted to see. Jesus was dead and they expected the worst (John 20:11, 19; Luke 24:1). They were astounded when he manifested himself.

The ability to give first-hand witness to the resurrection was the indispensable foundation of apostleship in the strict sense (Acts 1:22), but not all those to whom Jesus appeared became apostles. A further step was necessary, namely, a commission to preach.

Power as Proof

THE CORINTHIANS HAD to take Paul's word for it that he had seen the Risen Jesus. In the last analysis, however, it was a secondary issue. Apollos had not had such an experience. Nonetheless he was accepted as an authentic minister because he came with credentials from Ephesus (Acts 18:27). Thus it was much more important for Paul to prove that he had been commissioned to preach.

The community at Corinth had been founded when Paul was a missionary sent by the Church of Antioch. In the meantime, however, there had been a falling out (Galatians 2:11–14), and Antioch no longer approved of Paul's missionary practice. He refused to bow to its demand that pagans had to accept circumcision and the Jewish food laws in order to become Christians. It would have been futile to ask Antioch for credentials.

Paul therefore had to rely on the evidence of grace. Given his manifest lack of stature and resources, the very existence of the Church at Corinth demonstrated that divine power worked through him. The fact that Corinthians were Christians stamped Paul's ministry with the seal of authenticity.

PRAYER
Lord, grant that I may recognize true ministers, not by paper
qualifications or titles, but by the power of grace that they display.

COMPARISON WITH OTHERS

IN ORDER TO reject the authenticity of Paul's ministry the Corinthians must have had some standard with which to compare him. Only their awareness of a different style of ministry practiced by more eminent figures could serve as justification for his condemnation. If he did not use the advantages that others in his position enjoyed, it must be because he recognized that he had no right to them.

Paul had not realized that his renunciation of his right to support could be so misinterpreted. As we have already seen on a number of occasions, he tended to assume that what was clear to him would be clear to others. Now he was forced to recognize that, in order for his claim of renunciation to be reasonable, he had first to prove that he had the right.

A Familiar Phrase

IT IS UNDERSTANDABLE that Paul should explicitly mention the right of an apostle to food and drink. They were fundamental to everyone's survival. But why should he drag in the fact that other missionaries traveled with their wives? It was irrelevant to the point at issue. If they worked for the gospel, as so many women did (Romans 16:6–15), then of course they had the same claim to support as their male partners. More importantly, Paul was single when he wrote this and he had no intention of remarrying (7:6–9).

The answer to the question perfectly illustrates a facet of Paul's mentality. Eating and drinking were the first two parts of a well-known phrase whose third element was always a euphemism for sexual intercourse. "The people sat down to eat and drink and rose up to revel" (Exodus 32:6 cited in 1 Corinthians 10:7); "Eat, drink, and be merry" (Luke 12:19; cf. 2 Samuel 11:11). The mention of food and drink made Paul think of women and bed! He was an associative, lateral thinker. Inevitably his line of argument is not always what linear logicians expect.

Other Missionaries

CEPHAS WAS CERTAINLY married; it is the only way to acquire a mother-in-law (Mark 1:30). Paul may even have met Peter's wife when he stayed with him for two weeks in the autumn of A.D. 37 (Galatians 1:18). Who the "other apostles" were no one knows. Paul may have been thinking of the other missionaries who fanned out to the north and west from Antioch.

The only "brother of the Lord" to be mentioned by Paul is James, the eldest (15:7; Galatians 1:19). The other three were Joseph—better known as Joses—Simon, and Judas (Mark 6:3; Matthew 13:55). Some people think that these were sons of Joseph by a previous marriage. In the nonbiblical sources they are always older than Jesus, and he alone is called "the son of Mary" (Mark 6:3). This is the first reference to missionary activity of Jesus' brothers, but a contemporary source reveals that Nazareth was a missionary center of his relatives in the third century.

Barnabas was sent to Antioch from Jerusalem to steady a Church reeling under persecution (Acts 11:22). His recruitment of Paul, a converted persecutor, was a brilliant strategy to encourage a shaken Church (Acts 11:26). Subsequently Barnabas led Paul on a mission in Cyprus and southern Turkey (Acts 13:3). They eventually quarreled and parted (Acts 15:39), but some years later they stood together to defend the rights of pagan converts at the crucial meeting in Jerusalem in A.D. 51 (Galatians 2:9). Paul may have learned from Barnabas that only a needed skill gave missionaries financial independence. This, however, did not negate their right to support.

PRAYER

Lord, make all ministers worthy of their hire.

ARGUMENTS FOR SUPPORT

THE RHETORICAL QUESTIONS of the previous verses, which demand the answer Yes, clearly establish Paul's right to be supported by the communities for which he worked. He was so incensed, however, by the Corinthians' misunderstanding of his refusal to take money from them that he showered them with further arguments. The number of the reasons he gives implicitly highlights the slowness of the intellectuals whose "wisdom" had not brought them to the truth. Games are still being played, and Paul's resentment simmers beneath the surface.

The Laborer Is Worthy of His Hire

THE REASONS GIVEN earlier in this chapter could be interpreted to mean that Paul's right to support was based on his position in the Church. The individuals with whom he compares himself were all eminent figures. Now he has to make it clear that their claim to sustenance, as well as his, was based on what they contributed to the spread of the gospel. Support was not a privilege but a return for service.

Common sense furnished the opening arguments. No one sets up a vineyard without drinking the wine. No soldier pays himself to fight. No shepherd refrains from supplying his needs from his flock. Whatever the status of the individual, whether owner, employee, or slave, the principle is the same. Work merits reward (2 Timothy 2:6).

Just in case someone at Corinth might object that the principles of the world have no relevance to the ministry of the gospel, Paul invoked the authority of the Law. The citation from Deuteronomy 25:5 evokes the harvest scene of an ox pulling a nail-studded wooden sledge over the grain to separate the kernels from the stalks. If God cared enough for animals to exclude the use of a muzzle that would prevent the ox from nibbling the grain, he cannot have less concern for human beings. By extension, therefore, they too have the right to live from their labor.

Since Paul had brought the gospel to the Corinthians they owed him something. And they got the best of the bargain, because in exchange for the spiritual they could return only material goods. The only other person we know to have made a similar contribution to the Church at Corinth is Apollos (3:5–9), and he evidently was granted the right that Paul claimed.

Paul thought of his ministry in terms of service. He was graced by God "to be a minister of Christ Jesus to the Gentiles in the priestly service of the gospel of God" (Romans 15:16). Thus it was perhaps inevitable that he should invoke the way that temple servants, both Jewish and pagan, were supported.

A Commandment of the Lord

THE CLIMAX OF Paul's chain of arguments is "The Lord commanded those who proclaim the gospel to get their living from the gospel." Jesus in fact never gave such a command. He merely quoted a proverb, "The laborer deserves his wages/food" (Luke 10:7; Matthew 10:10). It is understandable, however, that this should have been interpreted as a principle controlling missionary activity. The force of the other arguments used by Paul, which were also available to others, explains why it became the rule.

What is really significant is that Paul understood the rule as laying an obligation on the preachers and not on their congregations. Ministers must accept support from their converts. They should not earn their own living but give themselves full-time to their ministry.

This final argument differs from all the others on one crucial point. They establish a "right," a privilege that may or may not be used, whereas it imposes an "obligation" that gives one no choice. Yet Paul reclassified it as optional, and decided that he was not going to accept it. Once again, as in the case of divorce (7:10–11), he refuses to recognize any command as a binding precept.

PRAYER

Lord, give me the courage to avoid the crutches of rules and regulations and to accept the responsibility of my decisions.

GOING HIS OWN WAY

PAUL'S CONVERSION CONVINCED him that God had chosen him to be an apostle to the Gentiles. This meant a lifetime of travel. How was he to support himself? To become the client of a rich person meant limiting his ministry to the guests of his patron. To become a wandering preacher who passed around the hat after each sermon would obscure what made the gospel special. There was only one option left. Even though it went against the grain of his elitist upbringing, he courageously learned a trade that gave him both mobility and financial independence.

A good tentmaker (Acts 18:3) accustomed to working in leather and canvas was welcomed by travelers and in towns and villages. Leather garments and harnesses, sails, and awnings needed repair as frequently as new ones were required. Problems arose when Paul had put a new community on its feet. Time that should have been devoted to his craft went to believers who needed his attention. His earnings dropped. At this point the money issue became critical.

Why Did Paul Not Ask for Support?

PAUL FELT THAT if he asked for financial assistance he would be putting an obstacle in the way of the gospel (9:12b). He feared that it would be a burden for the Thessalonians to support him (1 Thessalonians 2:9; 2 Thessalonians 3:8). The Church at Thessalonica was made up of manual laborers like himself, and he knew the financial pressures that blighted their lives. Would they refuse to accept the gospel if they knew that it would cost them hard-earned money?

The situation was different at Corinth where the Church had wealthy members (1:26). A request would have put them in no financial difficulty, but Paul was convinced that the gospel had to be given freely (9:18). He had to distinguish himself from the religious charlatans who faked miracles in order to enhance their income. He could not sell the gospel as they, in effect, sold their teachings. His generosity was evidence of the transformation that he claimed the word of God could effect (2:4). Paul felt he had no choice, and put the point across with a rare touch of humor. "What are the wages of one not entitled to any? Why, to do the work for free!" (9:18).

Why Did Paul Refuse What Was Offered?

IN PAUL'S WORLD, money in the bank was meaningless. It was changed into status and power by being distributed. A gift proclaimed superiority and demanded honor in return. Many at Corinth would have offered Paul support as a matter of course, for they automatically gained an enhanced position in both Church and society.

Paul, however, could not afford to accept the benefactions offered. The needy poor would have no chance against the resources of the wealthy, and how could he divide his time and energy among the latter? Not surprisingly he refused all gifts from the Corinthians. This angered those whose expectations of glory were thwarted.

Then, instead of telling the Corinthians that he was being subsidized by Philippi, and showing them that distance and a lump sum from a whole Church (see Philippians 4:15) ensured that he did not become a client of anyone, Paul insisted that he did not make *full* use of his right to support (9:18). By this he meant that he did not exercise his right at Corinth, but made *some* use of that right among the churches of Macedonia. Inevitably there was an explosion when the full truth was discovered (2 Corinthians 11:7–9).

PRAYER
Lord, as a minister make me ever obedient to your word, "Freely you have received, freely give" (Matthew 10:8).

ALL THINGS TO EVERYONE

IN THE LAST section we saw that Paul was conscious that his behavior was not consistent. He had founded the Church at Philippi and at Corinth. Members of both communities were able and willing to help him financially. But he accepted subsidies from the Philippians, while refusing support from the Corinthians. In order to undermine his authority, his enemies at Corinth would explain the difference by pointing out that obviously he loved the former and despised the latter.

What Is Integrity?

AT THIS STAGE Paul did not anticipate such a disastrous outcome, but he knew that he had to justify behavior that even his friends would find difficult to understand. He was never the same person twice. "All things to everyone" was a recipe for catastrophe. How could he be true to himself? Did he not have any integrity?

Paul took the question seriously, but transformed it. Unwilling, as always, to accept the standards of a fallen world, he reformulated the question in Christian terms: What is integrity for ministers of the gospel? Is it external or internal consistency? Is it related to their vision of themselves or to their effectiveness in their ministry?

Jews and Gentiles

THE MAJOR GROUPS with whom Paul had to deal were Jews and Greeks (1:24; 10:32; 12:13). He used this latter term to mean not merely the inhabitants of Greece, but pagans in general. Since the issue was his differing behavior toward the two groups, one would have expected him to follow his mention of "Jews" with a reference to "Greeks." Instead we find Jews redefined as "those under the Law (of Moses)" who he contrasts with "those outside the Law" (literally "the Law-less"), pagans to whom the Mosaic Law had not been given. Then without any warning he jumps to "the weak."

The shifts in argument and some of the language must have been rather disconcerting to his readers, who had reason to feel that they were being manipulated. For Paul to laugh up his sleeve in this way was a risky business, particularly when writing to a community that was already critical of him.

The fact that Paul had no scruple against accepting the social conventions of pagans, in order to get close enough to them to interest them in the gospel, underlines the extent to which he had broken with his Jewish past. The observances to which Jews clung fiercely in order to mark themselves as different from all other peoples, notably circumcision and the food laws, had become for Paul completely irrelevant. To adopt them or to ignore them was of no concern. Nothing now mattered but the imitation of Christ.

Paul therefore could play at being a Jew or a Gentile as it suited him. He does not use this language when speaking of the "weak." A reference to those who opposed the eating of idol meat (cf. 8:10–13) is probably embedded in a wider evocation of all who were socially and economically powerless. Paul was weak in this sense and nothing could change it. He was always the vulnerable outsider.

Christ the Law

THE QUARREL WITH Peter at Antioch (Galatians 2:11–14) revealed to Paul that to give the Law any place in a Christian community would lead inexorably to legalism. In reaction he repudiated the Law completely, not just in terms of its nationalistic Jewish identity markers (Acts 21:21), but precisely as law. There was no place in the Church for binding commandments. This left Paul open to the accusation of being "lawless," which, however, he anticipated and refuted by insisting that he was "under the law of Christ." This is not a new code, but the response to God's grace demanded by the self-sacrificing love of Christ. "Bear one another's burdens and so fulfill the law which is Christ" (Galatians 6:2).

PRAYER
God, grant that my personal preferences and inherited attitudes may never disrupt my ministry of the gospel or relationships with others.

SELF-DISCIPLINE

IN ANTIQUITY ATHLETES performed nude. Consequently, sporting activities were rejected by religious Jews. The construction of a gymnasium in Jerusalem was seen as an abomination (1 Maccabees 1:14; 2 Maccabees 4:9). Given the long years that Paul spent as a strictly observant Pharisee in Jerusalem (Galatians 1:14), one would not have expected him to be interested in sports. How far he had moved from a traditional Jewish stance is confirmed once again by his use here of running and boxing as metaphors of virtue. This is the first time that he has used such imagery, and it was undoubtedly inspired by what went on in Corinth in the spring of A.D. 51 when the Greek world gathered for the Isthmian Games.

The Isthmian Games

NO ONE TODAY living in a city preparing for or hosting the Olympic Games could be unaware of what was going on. The Isthmian Games had the same social and economic impact on Corinth, which hosted them every second year in the late spring. These games ranked third of the four great festivals that celebrated the unity of the Greek people, the others being the Olympic, Pythian, and Nemean Games. They took place at the temple of Poseidon, the god of the sea, at Isthmia some nine miles east of Corinth.

The foot races were always in multiples of 200 meters, the length of the track, and the longest was twelve laps. In races longer than a single length, runners had to make a sharp turn around a post in the middle of the finishing line. Strength and good elbows were almost as important as speed. Boxers' hands were bound with soft leather, both to protect the knuckles and to avoid cutting the opponent's face. In Paul's time winners were crowned with dry wild celery.

At Isthmia the sanctuary and racetrack were the only structures. There was no housing for the vast numbers of visitors. Corinth had to provide tents. Equally the shopkeepers who flocked out from the city to meet the needs of the visitors needed booths for their goods. The Isthmian Games were a godsend to the tentmakers of Corinth. The workshop of Prisca and Aquila in which Paul labored (Acts 18:1–3) would have been busy for months before and after. Presumably the various workshops sent craftsmen out to Isthmia during the games to effect repairs as they became necessary.

Sporting Metaphors

GIVEN THE INTIMATE connection between the tentmaking business and the Isthmian Games, it is impossible that Paul could have been ignorant of what went on at Isthmia. His reference to a perishable wreath reveals the precision of his knowledge. All the victors' crowns would eventually perish—the wild olive of the Olympic Games, the laurel of the Pythian Games, and the fresh wild celery of the Nemean Games—but only the Isthmian wreath was withered when it was presented.

The point that Paul wanted to convey by means of the athletic metaphor was that Christians should not be less serious about their commitment than were athletes. These do it for a moment of fame that lasts hardly longer than the victory crown. Christians can look forward to an eternal reward.

The Olympic Games set the standards for the other games, and it was mandatory that competitors in the Olympic Games had to be in serious training for the ten months preceding the festival. They could be disqualified if they broke training. The four-year cycle of the great games was: Year 1: Olympic and Isthmian; Year 2: Nemean; Year 3: Pythian and Isthmian; Year 4: Nemean. In other words, at least one of the four great games took place each year. First-class athletes had to be in perpetual training.

Typically, Paul concludes by revealing that he practiced what he preached. To avoid disqualification he had to maintain consistent self-discipline. Continuously he had to remember to put others before himself. Fasting or flagellation might appear to be implied by Paul's words, but nothing could be further from his intention. He looked outward, not inward.

PRAYER
Lord, make me singleminded in selflessness.

SPIRITUAL FOOD AND DRINK

THE COMPLACENT SEE only what they want to see. They feel secure because they limit themselves to what they can control. Reality, however, does not take lightly to being ignored. Inexorably it takes its revenge by forcing confrontations with the "other factors" illegitimately set aside.

Paul was not at all sure that he had succeeded in convincing the Strong (those who ate idol meat) that their sense of security had no basis. He knew the difficulty of trying to breach the wall of complacency that they had built around themselves. One line of attack was unlikely to be sufficient. A second had to be put in place. He decided to show them what had happened to others who prided themselves that they could not fall. They believed that their gifts were a guarantee that they would not be brought down.

Miracles of the Exodus

THE STORY OF the flight of the Israelites from Egypt is told in the book of Exodus. They had been enslaved by the Egyptians but, under the leadership of Moses, they broke out of captivity and headed for freedom in the Sinai desert. Every Jew knew the story in detail. It was retold every Passover.

The "cloud" symbolized the presence of God, "Yahweh [the Lord] preceded them, by day in a pillar of cloud to show them the way, and by night in a pillar of fire to give them light" (Exodus 13:21). As the fleeing Israelites halted at the edge of the Sea of Reeds and the Egytian chariot squadrons raced into the attack, "the pillar of cloud moved from their front and took position behind them. It came between the army of the Egyptians and the army of Israel . . . Then Moses stretched out his hand over the sea, and Yahweh drove the sea back with a strong easterly wind all night and made the sea into dry land. The waters were divided and the Israelites went on dry ground right through the sea, with walls of water to the right and left of them" (Exodus 14:19–22). When the sea rushed back, it destroyed the pursuing Egyptians.

The "spiritual" food was meat and manna. "That evening, quails flew in and covered the camp, and next morning there was a layer of dew all round the camp. When the layer of dew lifted, there on the surface of the desert was something fine and granular, as fine as hoarfrost on the ground" (Exodus 16:13–14). The "spiritual" water sprang from a rock when Moses struck it (Exodus 17:1–7). In popular belief the rock thereafter followed the Israelites, effectively serving as a water tank.

Paul then surprises us by saying "the rock was Christ." He certainly did not mean that Christ had been physically present in the form of a rock. Since the rock belonged to the past and Christ to the present, Paul had a choice of tenses in order to express the relationship. He could have said "the rock is Christ," but he preferred the past tense in order to force his readers to look backward.

Baptism and Eucharist

IN EFFECT PAUL is telling the Corinthians to put themselves in the place of the Israelites with whom they have so much in common. The Israelites went through something similar to Christian baptism. They ate spiritual food, as believers do in the eucharist. They had a rock as a continuous source of divine nourishment, just as Paul's converts have Christ. Nonetheless the Israelites displeased God, and were punished. Christians could suffer the same fate.

The vast majority of Corinthian Christians were not Jews. Yet Paul expected them to grasp the implications of his cryptic allusions to the exodus from Egypt. This means that a significant number of his pagan converts must have been "God-fearers," Gentiles who had been attracted by the austerity of Jewish monotheism and who went to the synagogue on Saturday to hear the scripture readings and sermons.

PRAYER

Lord, strip away my illusions of righteousness, and convince me of the
real nature of my security before you.

LEARNING FROM OTHERS' MISTAKES

"THEY WERE OVERTHROWN in the wilderness" (10:5). Paul's readers, of course, knew exactly what happened to the faithless Israelites. Of the 603,550 men aged twenty years and over and fit to bear arms who left Egypt, only two entered the Promised Land (Numbers 1:46; 14:30). They had desired evil and paid the price. Those today who "desire evil" will suffer the same way. But what exactly does "to desire evil" mean? Paul selects four examples from the exodus story that have particular relevance to the situation at Corinth.

Idolatry

PAUL PUTS "IDOLATRY" at the head of the list. Nothing we have seen so far suggested that any of the Corinthians had turned back from the one true God to idols. Some, however, had given the impression of being idolaters by eating a ritual meal in a pagan temple, and thereby had done the work of demons by destroying other members of the community (8:10–11; 10:20–21).

Paul quotes Exodus 32:6 because it contains the phrase "the people sat down to eat." He took it for granted that his audience would recall the context. The meal in question was the eating of the sacrifices that had been offered to the Golden Calf, the idol that Aaron had made when Moses was delayed on Mount Sinai (Exodus 32:1–6).

In this instance Paul assumes that his audience will remember the consequences of the worship of the Golden Calf. The Levites slaughtered 3,000, and others died in a plague (Exodus 32:28, 35). In the other three examples we have to work back to the incidents from the punishments. The knowledge of the scriptures that Paul presumes in his non-Jewish audience is exceptional; he seems to be expecting a lot of them.

Immorality

THE MENTION OF "immorality" in second place betrays the logic of a lateral, associative thinker, because "to dance" in the quotation from Exodus 32:6 is a euphemism for sexual activity.

Paul has already criticized the sexual morality of the Corinthians on several occasions. There had been incest (5:1–5), casual fornication (5:11), pederasty (6:9), and prostitution (6:15).

Paul's allusion to the death of 23,000 has given rise to a minor puzzle known as "The Case of the Missing Thousand." He can only be referring to the incident at Shittim where "the people gave themselves over to prostitution with Moabite women" (Numbers 25:1) with the result that "in the ensuing plague 24,000 of them had died." Paul's memory evidently was not as good as he expected that of his audience to be!

Testing God by Grumbling

THE ONE OCCASION in the scriptures where serpents carried out the punishment is: "The people spoke against God and against Moses, 'Why did you bring us out of Egypt to die in the desert? For there is neither food nor water here; we are sick of this meager diet.' At this God sent fiery serpents among the people; their bite brought death to many in Israel" (Numbers 21:5–6).

By joining the Church the Corinthians had left their comfortable world. Their sumptuous meals in pagan temples had been replaced by the austerity of bread and wine at the eucharist. No one, apparently, protested as overtly as the Israelites, but some did by their attitude. They continued to partake of ritual temple meals (8:10; 10:21). Whatever their intentions, or self-justification (8:1–4), Paul saw this as criticism of God's plan for the Christian community.

"The Destroyer" is the angel who killed the first-born children of the Egyptians (Exodus 12:23). He is invoked here as the supreme threat to those who murmur against God or his instruments on earth, one of whom was Paul.

PRAYER

Lord, grant that I may learn the lessons of history.

SCRIPTURE AND TEMPTATION

EVEN THOUGH PAUL, rightly or wrongly, took it for granted that the Corinthians had a rather detailed knowledge of the scriptures, their behavior brought it home to him that they had not seen the relevance to their own lives of what they had read. They appreciated the stories of the Israelites as history. They did not see them as mirrors in which they were reflected.

The Purpose of the Scriptures

THE CONTINUITY OF divine purpose was basic to Paul's worldview. God, he believed, had a plan for humanity that was being steadily worked out. The events of the exodus were part of that plan. The struggles in the desert had meaning and purpose. Through them the Israelites came to a realization of their destiny as God's chosen people and were made aware of the type of behavior that was demanded of them. They learned the lessons of often bitter experience.

The fact that their stories were written down, and passed on from generation to generation, indicated to Paul that they must have a purpose over and above the formation of the Israelites. They were meant to be read and pondered. The same triumphs and failures recur throughout the history of humanity. Believers should see the similarities between their circumstances and the lives of their ancestors in the faith. What were identified as mistakes in the past should be avoided in the present.

No Jew would have disagreed with this way of looking at the sacred scriptures. Paul, however, saw a special relation between the scriptures and himself and his Christian contemporaries. All of history had been designed by God to lead up to the moment of fulfillment in Christ. It was he who brought the divine plan to completion. Since the scriptures narrated the past with a view to the future, they must be of particular relevance to the last period of history in which Paul and his converts were living. The Church reaps the benefit of the experience of all past ages.

No Security

ONE OF THE most obvious lessons of the scriptures is that those who were most blessed by God regularly proved faithless and were punished. The Israelites could flatter themselves that they had been chosen by God and were protected by him. But this did not stop them from raising up a false god, the Golden Calf, and prostituting themselves with pagan women.

Although they had been admitted into the sphere of freedom where the power of sin could not touch them, the Corinthians had to learn that their behavior was not automatically good. They were in the process of being saved, but they had brought with them into the community all the bad habits they had acquired during their previous life. In the world such attitudes had been necessary to survival. One had to look out for number one because no one else did. Paul's converts had theoretically repudiated all forms of selfishness when they committed themselves to Christ, but Paul had enough experience to know that old habits die hard. Unless they were resisted, such habits would make conversion meaningless.

Christians therefore have to struggle to be true to the vision of genuine humanity revealed in Christ. They cannot take their freedom for granted. It has to be rewon every day (Galatians 5:1). The testing goes on and on. Paul does promise, however, that believers will not be overwhelmed. They will always have the choice of doing good. Their human dignity demands no less. They cannot be condemned despite themselves.

Paul bases this comforting view on the assumption that grace will always be available to strengthen and support those under pressure. Unfortunately this is not always true. Grace often comes through human channels. If believers are indifferent to one another they empty the cross of Christ of its power (1:17), and his saving grace does not arrive where it is required. The weak who fall because they are unaided cannot be blamed.

PRAYER
Lord, help me learn from the scriptures that I am the channel of grace which makes it possible for others to resist temptation.

CHRISTIAN AND JEWISH SACRIFICES

AS FAR AS Paul was concerned, eating meat offered to idols was not evil in itself. It became wrong only in certain specific circumstances. We have already dealt with the case of a Christian who did not want to eat such meat but was pressured into doing so by an invitation that left him with no excuses (8:10–13). This situation arose because the Strong at Corinth considered themselves justified in eating meals in pagan temples. In their view these were purely social occasions, which in no way implied that they worshiped such gods.

The Consequences of Sociability

WE HUMANS ARE social creatures, and necessarily develop codes by which we communicate with each other. A combination of four letters could be given any meaning, but once one is established it must be socially accepted. An effort to redefine "fool" as "wise" would get nowhere.

Similarly we give social gestures specific meanings. A kiss is a sign of love, which is why its abuse, as in the case of Judas, is so abominable. A shared meal is a symbol of hospitality, of complete acceptance. Anyone who declared an invitation to a meal to be a sign of hate would be looked at very curiously, as would anyone who claimed that an attempt to claw his eyes out was a gesture of love.

Physical gestures cannot be given an arbitrary meaning. They say something in and of themselves which is independent of the intention of the person making the gesture.

Paul argued on this basis earlier regarding sexual intercourse (6:15–20). The sex act was intended to bind two people together permanently as one flesh. The customer of a prostitute had no right to impose his own subjective meaning that the act was transitory and insignificant. The act in itself made a statement that he had no authority to contradict. In that instance Paul concluded, "Flee fornication" (6:18).

Here he argues on the same basis with respect to participation in ritual meals in a pagan temple, and concludes, "Flee from idolatry" (10:14). First of all, however, he has to establish common ground with those who disagree with him.

What Happens at the Eucharist?

PAUL BEGINS BY stating what he can take for granted, presumably because he had taught the Corinthians the meaning of the eucharistic meal. Since no one had ever raised questions about it, with good reason he took silence for tacit acceptance. Thus he assumes that the Strong admitted the identification with Christ of the bread and wine over which the eucharistic words were spoken (11:23–25), and that they conceded that their participation in the eucharistic meal produced something. Otherwise, why would the practice continue? This is the common ground on which the argument depends.

The eucharistic ritual produces something, which Paul describes as *koinonia*. This word is best translated by "common union" (rather than "participation" or "sharing") because there is a double point of reference. Through sharing in the body and blood of Christ, believers are united with him *and* with one another. Since all share in the one drink which is Christ, and in the one bread which is Christ, Christ becomes a source of common sustenance which forges the believers into "one body." It is the organic unity of a living being, whose head and feet differ but share a common existence. Similarly the members of Christ's body coexist while retaining their distinctive identities.

For Jewish converts and those who had frequented the synagogue, Paul reinforces his point by a reference to the Jewish sacrifice of communion in which the victim was divided between God, the priests, and the offerers (1 Samuel 9:10–24). The meal brought all three together. Their sharing created a common union. They were changed by participation.

PRAYER

Lord, may my participation in the eucharist result in the formation of a genuine community with those who share the body and blood of Christ with me.

PAGAN SACRIFICES

HAVING SET THE stage by reminding the Strong of their understanding of the implications of participation in the eucharist and Jewish sacrifices, Paul finally comes to his main point. Whatever the Strong think they are doing, their participation in pagan temple meals has a necessary consequence that is built into the act. Their physical stance makes them "idolaters."

Christian and Pagan Sacrifices

PAUL COULD ANTICIPATE the Strong denying that there was any similarity between the eucharist or Jewish sacrifices and pagan meals. They had already stated their belief that there was only one God, and that idols did not really exist (8:4). Sacrifices offered to a real being, the Christian and Jewish God, were obviously different from sacrifices offered to a nonentity, and so the consequences for the participants must be different.

The "common union" resulting from Christian and Jewish sacrifice had both vertical and horizontal dimensions. It established a relationship with God and with the other participants. The Strong assumed that the lack of a vertical dimension in pagan sacrifices meant that the horizontal dimension was also missing. Their arrogance, however, had blinded them to the fact that this conclusion was manifestly false. The sharing of a ritual meal established a bond with the other guests. That was the very nature of the meal. Despite their intention the Strong had entered into a union with pagans whose belief gave a subjective existence to false gods.

More importantly, from Paul's perspective, the Strong had not thought through the vertical dimension properly. They were perfectly correct in insisting that no matter how much veneration was accorded a statue of Aphrodite, there was no correspondingly beautiful woman in the sky who made possible love, beauty, and fertility. But they had failed to recognize that behind the tawdry images of non-gods lurked "demons." Pagan sacrifices, in consequence, were offered to "demons" (Deuteronomy 32:17;

Psalm 106:37). The Strong who shared in such sacrifices by eating some of the meat that had been offered on the altar necessarily entered into a "common union," not only with their pagan friends but also with "demons."

Demons

IN SPEAKING OF "demons" Paul adopts the language of his contemporaries. Most religions in antiquity believed that illness and natural catastrophes were caused by malevolent nonhuman forces. Humans attempted to domesticate these powers by personalizing them. They thought of them as spiritual beings, "demons," to whom very often they gave names. Thus, it was believed, they could be warded off by incantations, or expelled by exorcisms. The absolute authority of Jesus over "demons" was one of the most striking features of his ministry (Matthew 8:28–34).

To what extent Paul shared the popular belief is difficult to say. This is the only passage in which he speaks of "demons," and he does so in a way that severely reduces the supernatural element that many like to exaggerate because it makes excuses easy to find—"A demon made me do it."

Paul's thought moves on a much more practical level. The Strong, he says, made themselves "partners with demons." He knew this theoretically from his understanding of pagan sacrifices, but he also knew it from the consequences of the actions of the Strong. Through their arrogance they destroyed other Christians (8:11). In other words, they accomplished the goal of the powers of evil. In practice they acted as "demons."

Only this aspect of demonology interested Paul. He saw it as one more illustration of the fact that in the real world good and evil work through human instruments. Without human cooperation both God and "demons" are powerless. God relies on people to mediate his grace to others (3:5–9). The false value-system of society, which Paul calls "sin" (Romans 3:9), is the tool used by the forces of evil to destroy humanity.

PRAYER
Lord, give me the insight and imagination to anticipate that my actions may have repercussions on the lives of others that I did not intend.

THE OTHER SIDE OF THE COIN

THERE ARE TWO sides to every issue, and eating meat offered to idols was no exception. At Corinth there were those who ate such meat and those who refused. Paul has devoted considerable space to dealing with the former, whose position he criticized firmly. This does not mean that the latter were exempt from blame. The Weak who refused to eat rather enjoyed their scruples, and projected them onto the Strong in a way that Paul found equally un-Christian.

An Emotional Reaction

PAUL HAD NO difficulty in understanding that some Christians were emotionally incapable of assimilating the teaching on monotheism to which they had assented intellectually at baptism. The previous lives of the Weak had been so dominated by belief in the gods who inhabited the temples with which Corinth abounded that, in their heart of hearts, they could not dismiss them as lightly as others in the community did.

The Weak were in an embarrassing position. Intellectually they denied the existence of idols, but emotionally they continued to believe in them. They must have been conscious of the contradiction, but they could do nothing about it. They could not deny their baptismal commitment, but neither could they simply tell their emotions to go away. Emotions are beyond rational control. For many people the knowledge that airplanes are one of the safest means of travel has no effect on their fear of flying.

To be in an indefensible position is extremely uncomfortable, and it is natural to look for a means of relieving the tension. One way is to assume that all others are in the same situation but do not have the courage to admit it. Another way is to lash out at those thought to be responsible for the situation. The first option does not exclude the second, and there are clear hints that the Weak adopted both.

An Attack on the Strong

THE WEAK COULD not bring themselves to believe that the Strong were acting in good faith. It must be said that the arrogance of the Strong, and the suffering that they had unwittingly caused, did not make it easy for the Weak to react charitably. As far as the Weak were concerned, the Strong were dominated by their craving for meat. Deep down, the Weak believed, the Strong knew that eating idol meat was wrong, yet the appeal of cheap meat outweighed the pangs of conscience that they certainly felt. In the eyes of the Weak, the Strong were hypocrites. In the strange way the mind operates, this made the Weak feel better about themselves. To criticize others relieved their own misgivings. They might have their problems, but at least they did not deceive themselves as the Strong did.

Paul found such smugness intolerable. He disagreed with the Strong, and felt that they should have been much more perceptive, but he did not believe that they had acted out of malice. They should have known better but their mistake was an honest one. The Strong were objectively wrong, but the Weak were equally blameworthy insofar as they projected what they felt onto others. "What good does it do for my freedom to be subjected to the judgment of another's conscience?" (10:29). To assume the worst about others is not Christian.

Paul was aware that perfectionists like to pry, and can make life miserable for everyone. Thus he insists that the Weak should not go looking for trouble by asking questions as to where meat came from, even when it was offered in a pagan house. Ignorance meant an easy conscience. If, however, a pagan fellow-guest, knowing the scruples of Christians and Jews, should point out that the meat on the table had been sacrificed, then the believer should abstain in order not to offend someone trying to be helpful.

PRAYER
God, help me to understand that many who oppose progress in the Church do so not out of ignorance or malice, but because of a gut feeling over which they have no control.

WITNESS TO THE WORLD

IN THE MOMENT of his conversion Paul became not only a Christian but an apostle. He became convinced that his way of being a Christian was to spread the gospel. As a result he thought of everything in missionary terms. The Church, therefore, did not exist for itself but for the world. It was not simply an association of those who were followers of Christ. It was primarily the instrument chosen by God to proclaim the good news of salvation, not only in word but in deed. Its role was to demonstrate to the world the values of which the gospel spoke.

Witness

THE CONDUCT OF both Strong and Weak at Corinth struck at the roots of the Church's mission. They behaved in a way which gave no hint that they had committed themselves to a new way of life. The confidence of the Strong in their intelligence, and their insistence on using what they considered to be their right, mirrored the complacent selfishness of society. The malice of the Weak, and their determination to believe the worst of their fellow believers, aligned them with their pagan contemporaries.

Not surprisingly, therefore, Paul insists that believers, in everything they do, should give glory to God. He is thinking not of prayer but of action. It is easy to mouth words and both Weak and Strong prayed together, with hatred in their hearts. Paul wants a complete change in their conduct. Just as a craftsman is honored by the perfection of his product, so God is glorified if believers are what he intended them to be; if their behavior is modeled on that of Christ, who gave himself in love (Galatians 2:20) that humans might no longer live for themselves (2 Corinthians 5:15).

The translation "give no offense to Jews or Greeks" can be read as if Paul merely intended that believers should put no obstacles in the way of any outsider who inquired about the faith of Christians. The reference to his own example shows that Paul intended a much more positive attitude (see Philippians 2:14–16). He wanted to win converts, which meant reaching out in an effort to "please" everyone with whom he comes in contact.

Once again Paul appears to contradict himself. It is clear from the context that "to please" here means "to attract," but he regularly used "to please" in a different sense: "We speak, not to please men, but to please God" (1 Thessalonians 2:4; see Galatians 1:10). Paul did not tailor his preaching to the desires of his hearers in order to curry favor with them. On the contrary, he strove to make the gospel attractive by the quality of his conduct. One of his followers will speak of such behavior as "beautifying" the word of God (Titus 2:10).

Imitation

PAUL HAD A very precise answer for those who asked, "What does being a Christian mean?" He simply said, "Look at me, and imitate what I do." This might appear arrogant, as if he reduced the gospel to his own abilities. In fact Paul had no choice. The unspoken question in the minds of all was, "Is God's grace available *here and now?*" It could be answered only by proof, not by words. To talk about Christ would prove nothing because he could no longer be seen. Paul had to accept the responsibility of demonstrating the truth of the gospel by inviting people to see the present power of grace transforming him. He had to be another Christ (2 Corinthians 4:10–11).

The ability to answer in this way is the true test of authentic ministry. It cuts across all linguistic and cultural barriers in a way that paper qualifications never can. To every community that knew him personally, Paul summarized his message by "Imitate me" (1 Corinthians 4:16; Galatians 4:12; Philippians 3:17; 1 Thessalonians 1:6; 2:14; 2 Thessalonians 3:7–9).

PRAYER
O God, may I beautify the word of God by my every action.

A NEW VISION OF HEADSHIP

FROM THE WAY Paul formulates 11:2 we can deduce that the Corinthians concluded the section of their letter dealing with idol meat more or less in the following words: "Even though we disagree on the question of idol meat, on which you gave us no directions, nonetheless we remember everything you told us, and we maintain the traditions just as you gave them to us. In particular we come together for prayer and the celebration of the eucharist."

Talking Down to Paul

THE TONE BETRAYS the self-satisfaction of the Corinthians. The Strong had solved a tricky problem by decisive reasoning, and expected Paul's approval. They had taken responsibility for their own lives, and thereby showed him that they could get on without him. Nonetheless, they graciously assured him, he had not been forgotten.

How the community was feeling by the time they got to this point in the public reading of 1 Corinthians is best left to the imagination. Even though Paul may not have convinced either the Strong or the Weak, he had certainly shattered their complacency. Now, while they are still reeling, he delivers further hammer blows by finding fault with aspects of their assemblies for worship.

A Forgotten Source of Information

PAUL HAD BEEN away from Corinth for over three years. What he knew about the affairs of the community, the Corinthians assumed, came from the letter they wrote (1 Corinthians 7:1) and the official delegation that brought it to Ephesus (1 Corinthians 16:17). These were two official sources of information, and inevitably focused on unresolved problems.

There were other areas of community life, however, on which there was no disagreement—for example, public prayer, the eucharist, and the liturgical use of the gifts of the Spirit. The Corinthians considered they had no need to go into details about such matters. It sufficed to mention them as areas of consensus. General agreement in a community so diverse was seen as a guarantee that they must be on the right track.

Paul, however, had a third source of information that the Corinthians had forgotten about. These were the employees of Chloe (1:11) who, after a business trip to Corinth, returned to Ephesus with vivid stories of the bizarre behavior of the members of the Church they had visited. Paul was so shocked at what the Corinthians accepted without any problems that he immediately sent Timothy to find out if the report was true. Before his return, the delegation from Corinth arrived. Chloe's people had provided Paul with the questions to ask, and he surprised the delegates into confirming what he suspected regarding their public assemblies.

Headship

BEFORE EVEN INDICATING what the first problem was, Paul felt constrained to establish a guiding principle in which he defines three sets of relationships—man–Christ, woman–man, Christ–God—in terms of "head." This word has a wide variety of meanings in English, virtually all of which convey the notion of superiority. This is clear in "head of state" or "headmaster," but also in cases where "head" evokes the upper part of a nail, cane, sail, staircase, etc. Thus, the relationships have been understood hierarchically: Christ is superior to every human being. Man is superior to woman. God is superior to Christ.

In Greek, however, the instances where "head" implies superiority are very rare. Much more commonly it means "source," and this is the meaning demanded by the context (11:8) for the second pair here. In the account of creation, woman is drawn from man (Genesis 2:21). This obliges us to interpret the other two relationships in the same way. Christ is the source of the new life of every believer; "man" here evidently includes women. God is the source of Christ's existence as Son of God. The text therefore cannot be used as scriptural proof of the inferiority of women. On the contrary, the bracketing of a relationship founded on the first creation by relationships derived from the new creation (2 Corinthians 5:17) hints at a Christian revision of the status of women.

PRAYER
Lord, grant that every authority may be a source of life.

A HAIRY PROBLEM

HAIR HAS ALWAYS been a sensitive issue. Those with long memories will remember the storm that arose between the two world wars when women began to cut their hair short. The reaction was as violent as it was irrational. It stemmed from a deep revulsion, the sense that a law of nature had been violated, that something profoundly important had been challenged. Of course, as time went on, things calmed down and short hair on women was taken for granted. An identical crisis, however, developed in the 1960s when men started to let their hair grow long. The same cries of outrage were heard, reminding us that hair has the capacity to trigger an emotional response. The same type of situation developed at Corinth.

Long Hair on Men

FOR MANY STUDENTS of this letter the problem, as far as male believers were concerned, was that they covered their heads at worship. No good reason has been given why Paul should object to such a practice. In fact he should have favored it, because every priest in what he believed to be the true religion officiated wearing a head covering (Exodus 28:36–40; 39:28; Ezekiel 44:18).

The texts, however, never mention headgear. The first condemns a man for "having something hanging from his head" (11:4). The natural interpretation that this means "long hair" is confirmed by the second reference, "A man who wears his hair long dishonors himself" (11:14). Why should the length of a man's hair be an issue?

In Paul's world, for a man to attach too much importance to the way his hair was dressed hinted at effeminacy, at sexual ambiguity. If he let his hair grow long, it proclaimed his homosexuality both for Jews and for Gentiles. The Roman Juvenal speaks dismissively of "a long-haired catamite" (*Satires* 8:130), whereas the Jewish philosopher Philo rails against homosexuals because of "the provocative way they curl and dress their hair" (*The Special Laws* 3:36). Hair was grown long in order to create a feminine hairdo. The normal hair length for men was the short-back-and-sides that one sees on Roman statues of the period. For Jews the standard was set by the priests: "They shall not shave their heads or let their locks grow long; they shall only trim the hair of their heads" (Ezekiel 44:20).

Disordered Hair on Women

PAUL AGREES WITH his contemporaries that long hair on a woman is her crowning glory. But he adds, "for her hair is given to her as a wrapper" (11:15). The meaning of "wrapper" becomes clear from female statues of the period. Women plaited their hair and coiled it around the top of their heads to create a little hair cap. This common hairstyle is the "covering" of which Paul speaks. He is not thinking of a "veil." The word never occurs in this chapter.

There were women converts at Corinth who did not dress their hair in the conventional fashion. Presumably they let it flow loosely. There is no evidence that this suggested deviant sexuality. Paul, however, brings it into line with the case of the man. If the woman is not prepared to be feminine, he says, then she might as well go the whole way and be "mannish." Lesbians shaved their heads to be comfortable when wearing wigs, or else cut it short as men did. Lucian describes a woman "with her hair closely clipped in the Spartan style, boyish-looking and quite masculine" (*The Runaways*, 27).

Childish Corinthians

THIS SITUATION SHOWED the Corinthians at their childish best. Paul had told them "there is neither Jew nor Greek, neither slave nor free, *neither male nor female*" (Galatians 3:28). In response they decided that the difference between the sexes should be canceled! It was their way, together with approving incest (5:1–5), of standing out from their environment. Such misinterpretation of his words drove Paul frantic.

PRAYER
Lord, let me not be swayed by the prejudices of my contemporaries.

Using Scripture

The situation in the liturgical assemblies at Corinth, where the men looked like women and the women looked awful, disturbed Paul, not merely because of its absurd childishness but because he did not know whether homosexual appearances were associated with homosexual practices. Chloe's people would not have been in a position to know, and it was not the sort of question he could put to an official delegation from the Church. He thus had to be very careful in how he dealt with the problem. It would ruin his credibility to accuse the Corinthians of something that they were not guilty of.

How Men and Women Should Dress Their Hair

Paul structures his argument here in a curious way. Instead of first expounding the scripture on which his case rests, and then drawing the appropriate conclusions, he separates the two conclusions (11:7 and 10) by the text from Genesis.

What Paul wants the men to do is perfectly clear. They should not "cover" their heads while praying or prophesying. He has defined "cover" in the previous section as meaning the normal feminine hairdo in which long plaits were coiled around the top of the head to create a hair cap. In other words, as far as his hair is concerned, a man should look like a man.

One would expect Paul's conclusion regarding women to be identical. And in fact it is, but this is not apparent in any translation. For centuries this passage has been read as a reproof addressed to women who would not accept divinely ordained male superiority, and a statement appropriate to this approach has been substituted for Paul's words; for example, "a woman ought to have a veil on her head" (Revised Standard Version) as a sign of subjection.

The most literal translation of Paul's words in 11:10 is "a woman should exercise control over [her] head," and the most natural meaning is that she should dress her hair in the conventional manner. A woman who did not do her hair properly was failing to control it.

To the conclusion regarding the woman Paul adds, "because of the angels." It is natural to think of supernatural beings, but the most extraordinary speculation has been required to explain how they come into the picture. "Angel," however, merely means messenger, and the New Testament uses it to mean human envoys (e.g., Matthew 11:10). If we understand this sense to be the one here, everything falls into place. Paul did not want women with weird hairdos scandalizing visitors from other churches.

The Scriptural Argument

PAUL'S ARGUMENT IS based on Genesis 2:18–23 which describes the creation of Eve from the rib taken from the side of Adam in fulfillment of God's decision: "I will make him a helper as his partner." Paul makes the implications of this statement explicit: "Man was not created for woman, but woman for man." Thus woman gives glory to man, whereas man gives glory to God, whose image he is.

The idea of "glory" does not appear in the creation story, in which both man and woman are made in the image of God (Genesis 1:27). At first sight, therefore, Paul could be accused of having exaggerated the position of men in relation to women, but this could be said only by taking these verses out of their context.

The conclusions that Paul derives from the Genesis account determine what he saw in the text. As we have seen, he concludes only that men should look like men and women like women. The text, as he read it, emphasized only that men and women were *different*. Thus what he says must be designed to highlight the insight of Genesis that man and woman were not created in the same way. Hence, the difference between them was intended by God and must be respected.

PRAYER

Lord, help me to read the scriptures in order to be instructed, not to find confirmation for my prejudices.

WOMEN FULLY EQUAL

PAUL'S INTERPRETATION OF Genesis 2:18–23 could have been expressed more clearly. It might have been better had he formally stated how he read the text, instead of forcing his readers to work it out from his conclusions. Fortunately he was aware that he might be misunderstood, and took precautions that at least the worst possible interpretation could not be given to his words.

A False Reading of Genesis

WE HAVE ALREADY noted in several places both that the Corinthians were gifted misinterpreters of Paul, and that the fault was sometimes his own. Without being aware of it, he sometimes wrote in a way that permitted different interpretations, and was shocked when the Corinthians invariably took the meaning that he did not intend.

Even if Paul was not conscious of the ambiguity of his formulation here, he knew that there was a very real danger that his readers would not grasp his meaning. Even though the number of Jews in the Corinthian Church was minimal, a large number of believers had been associated with the synagogue before becoming Christians. In the Jewish tradition, Genesis 2:18–23 was used to prove the subordination of women. Since they had been created in second place after Adam, they could never occupy more than a second-class position. According to the first-century Jewish historian Josephus, "The woman, says the Law, is in all things inferior to the man. Let her accordingly be submissive" (*Against Apion* 2:200). Many of those hearing Paul's letter read aloud would immediately and instinctively bring this interpretation of Genesis to their understanding of Paul's words in 11:7–9. This is why he had to exclude it explicitly.

The Jewish argument for male superiority was based on chronological priority. Man was created first. This Paul cannot deny, but he turns the argument on its head by directing attention to the present, where chronological priority belongs to the woman. Every man comes from a woman's womb. And this arrangement, Paul points out, is just as much part of God's plan for humanity as the order of creation itself. The principle of who comes first, therefore, leads to contradictory conclusions and should be scrapped as meaningless.

Paul uses this irrefutable argument to sustain the earliest formal statement of the full equality of women: "As Christians, woman is not otherwise than man, and man is not otherwise than woman" (11:11). The emphatic "as Christians" implies a contrast between believers and others. Conversion does not make a woman equal to a man, but by becoming a Christian she leaves a world that considers her inferior and enters a community in which her innate equality is recognized. This, of course, was one of the factors that drew women to Christianity in the first century.

Praying and Prophesying

THE FULL EQUALITY of women in the life of the Church is evident from the very beginning of this section. Paul had trouble with the way some men and women at Corinth did their hair, but none with the fact that a woman prayed and prophesied in precisely the same way as a man (11:4–5). It is most revealing of the ethos of the Pauline communities that he took this entirely for granted. It was not something that he had to fight for.

In this context, praying and prophesying imply leadership roles in the Church. Prayer, of course, can be private, but in that case it would not matter how one's hair was done. Paul is thinking rather of the inspired prayer spoken out loud that brought a new theological insight to the attention of the assembled community. Prophecy was also inspired speech but designed for "the upbuilding, encouragement and consolation" of believers (14:3). It was the spiritual gift that brought to light and sustained all other divine gifts.

PRAYER
Lord, may all members recognize the full equality of women in every aspect of the Church's life.

SCANDALOUS SELFISHNESS

THE ATTEMPT ON the part of some Corinthians to blur the distinction between the sexes in the name of missionary witness was childish in the extreme. Paul found it shocking, but what really dismayed him was the fact that no one did anything about it. The majority of the believers accepted it, and may even have taken a certain pride in such eccentric behavior. Their tolerance, unfortunately, also extended to another much more serious aspect of the Church's liturgical life. They ignored radical discrimination at the eucharistic assembly. How could this have arisen?

The Corinthian Community

WE KNOW MORE about individual members of the Church at Corinth than any other of his foundations. Paul makes no attempt to give a complete list, but for various reasons sixteen certain names are scattered through three different sources: 1 Corinthians 16:17–19; Romans 16:1, 21–23; Acts 18:7–8, 17. We know that Prisca and Aquila were husband and wife, and must assume that all the others were married. Hence, fifteen couples, some of whom were converted with their households—the extended family plus servants. Thus there were at least forty to fifty people in the community at a conservative estimate.

The importance of this number becomes evident when it is related to the size of the dining room of an average upper-class house. The dining rooms at the temple of Asclepius (see 8:10–13) measured 7.11 × 7.11 yards, that is 50.55 square yards. This was the standard size. The only house from the time of Paul that has been excavated at Corinth is the villa at Anaploga. The quality of its magnificent mosaic floors show it to have been the home of a wealthy person. Its dining room measures 6.0 × 8.2 yards, that is 49.2 square yards.

Either of these rooms could contain the whole community provided that they stood closely together and each person occupied approximately one square yard—not a very comfortable or convenient arrangement for a liturgy. Moreover, there were couches along the walls, and diners expected to recline on them.

Simple logistics dictated the formation of subgroups that met in different homes, such as that of Prisca and Aquila (16:19). This, of course, facilitated the development of different theologies within the Church. To hold the community together it was imperative to have regular meetings of the "whole Church" (14:23). This is where the trouble began.

A Eucharist in the House of Gaius

LET US IMAGINE what happened when Gaius hosted the "whole church" (Romans 16:23). He would know that his dining room could not contain all the believers, so he had chairs set up in the courtyard around which ran a covered gallery. This arrangement immediately divided those who attended into first- and second-class members. Not only was it more prestigious to have a place in the dining room, but it was a lot more comfortable. It could be heated in winter, whereas the courtyard offered only cold drafts.

Who got invited into the dining room? One does not have to be very cynical to envisage Gaius saying to Christians of the same social bracket, "Look, if you get here a little early, you'll be sure of a place in the dining room, and we can have a couple of drinks and nibble a little until the others come and the celebration starts." He might need the same favor on another occasion. Slaves and others who had no control over their time would arrive much later, exhausted and hungry, to find that the better-off members of the community had eaten and drunk perhaps too well.

In Paul's eyes such blatant lack of love for the disadvantaged in the community meant that no eucharist was possible. The community might go through the motions and mouth the eucharistic words, but it could never be the Lord's supper (11:20). It would be better for the Corinthians to eat in their own houses rather than pretend to a unity that their behavior denies.

PRAYER
Lord, make me aware that love is necessary to the validity of the eucharist.

THE MEANING OF THE EUCHARIST

THE CONTEMPTUOUS TREATMENT of the "have-nots" at Corinth by wealthy believers scandalized Chloe's people. It is they who reported the practice to Paul. In showing his awareness of what went on, Paul's tone and harsh rhetorical questions make it abundantly clear that he shared the reaction of his informants. He goes further and asserts that the attitude of the Corinthians made a genuine eucharist impossible. He now has to justify that judgment.

The Institution of the Eucharist

PAUL FOUNDS HIS argument on the words pronounced over the bread and wine at the eucharistic celebration. He reveals his detailed knowledge of the gospel tradition by noting that the Last Supper took place the same night that Judas handed over Jesus to his enemies. Jesus was arrested in the garden of Gethsemane at the foot of the Mount of Olives on his way back to his lodgings with Martha, Mary, and Lazarus in Bethany.

There are four versions of the words spoken by Jesus at the Last Supper, all slightly different. Just to read them together reveals that they fall into two groups. Matthew (26:26–28) is very similar to Mark (14:22–24), whereas Paul's account resembles that of Luke (22:19–20). It is widely believed that Luke's version represents the liturgical usage of the Church of Antioch, which had been Paul's mother church until its decision to be a Jewish (rather than a Gentile) church forced him to leave.

Paul's version is virtually identical with that of Luke except for the ending, where he inserts a second command about "remembrance." Luke has only one. This Paul did to point up the radical contrast between the meaning of the rite and what went on at Corinth. The wealthy had forgotten what they were about, and reduced the eucharist to the level of an ordinary meal where it was taken for granted that the "haves" were treated in quite a different way from the "have-nots" in regard to both accommodations and food. If they ever thought of the self-giving of Jesus as displayed in his sharing of the bread and wine, it was as an event of the distant past without relevance to their situation.

What Does Real Remembrance Involve?

IN THE COMMENTARY (11:26) that Paul attaches to the words of institution, he makes it clear that real "remembrance" is something much more than an intellectual glance backward into the past. It is an existential statement which makes present the reality of Christ's love.

The "proclamation" that Paul has in mind is not verbal. It is not a retelling of the Passion of Jesus. The proclamation takes place in and through the ritual acts of eating and drinking. These acts, as we know from 10:14–18, are a sharing of bread and wine which produces a "common union" with Christ and the other participants. The eating and drinking "say" that the community is one, and that it is Christ, whose words are used in the first person singular. More than that, the sharing "proclaims" the Lord's death. For Paul this death was above all an act of love for others. Jesus chose the horrible death of crucifixion (Philippians 2:8) in order to demonstrate the limitless love that animated his self-giving (Galatians 2:20). The community can "proclaim" that love only by actually loving each other as Christ loved us.

This is what the eucharist meant to Paul. It was anything but a boring ritual. It was a mini-drama which restaged the dying of Jesus as a sharing in love that reflected his gift of self for others.

None of this was true at Corinth. The participants no doubt ate the same bread and drank the same wine, but there was no real sharing because there was no caring. The community was not animated by the love that would make it Christ—"to put on Christ" (Galatians 3:27) is "to put on love" (Colossians 3:14)—and so lost the power to say "This is *my* body/blood."

PRAYER
Lord, help me to ensure that the community with which I celebrate the eucharist is truly Christ-like.

PREPARING FOR THE EUCHARIST

PAUL'S RESPONSE TO the scandalous selfishness of some Corinthians was to explain the meaning of the eucharist. The community must be Christ-like in the sense that the members actually love one another if their eucharist is to be genuine. What were the Corinthians actually doing when they attempted to celebrate a loveless eucharist?

Murder!

PAUL WITHOUT HESITATION makes them guilty of the body and blood of the Lord. "To be guilty of the blood of someone" is to be liable for the death of that person. The author of the Epistle to the Hebrews, although speaking of another sin, brings out perfectly what Paul has in mind here: "They crucify the Son of God on their own account and hold him up to contempt" (6:6).

If those who participate in the eucharist do not act out in their sharing the saving love shown by Christ in his dying, then they are the murderers who stand around the cross sneering at their victim.

The brutally explicit formulation of this judgment was designed to shock the Corinthians into a realization of what they were doing. Paul also reinforces his point by showing them that God is not mocked. A farcical eucharist has frightening consequences.

There had been an unusually high number of deaths and illnesses in the community at Corinth. What the cause was we do not know, presumably one of the many infections with which the port cities of the eastern Mediterranean teemed, and which occasionally flared up into an epidemic. In any case Paul interprets this situation as a divine judgment on the community as a whole. His Jewish background would have made him familiar with the idea that sin and sickness were intimately related (Mark 2:1-12; John 9:1-2). He does not say, however, that those who were most guilty were punished most severely. The whole community had gone along with the fiction of sharing, and so the community as such suffered.

Self-Examination

IF AN ATTEMPT to celebrate the eucharist in a group that was a community only in name caused one to rank among the murderers of Jesus, then it was obvious that the assembled believers needed to check themselves carefully before embarking on a course that had such horrendous consequences.

What should they look for among themselves? What criterion should they use in judging? Paul's answer (11:29) needs to be read carefully.

The "eating" and "drinking" obviously refer to the consumption of the blessed bread and wine during the eucharist. It condemns those who do so "without discerning the body." This is the standard against which all must measure themselves. But what does "body" mean here?

Were the reference to the body of Christ under the species of bread, one would expect a parallel reference to the blood of Christ under the species of wine, particularly since Paul twice emphasizes "eating" *and* "drinking." Paul, therefore, does not make the criterion an ability to distinguish the eucharist from an ordinary meal.

The only alternative, since "body" alone is mentioned, is to take "body" as meaning the community. If Paul's conventions of writing were the same as ours, he would have written "Body" in order to indicate that he had in mind the Body of Christ. He presumed that his readers would remember what he had written in his allusion to the eucharist in the previous chapter, *"we who are many are one body,* for we all partake of the one bread" (10:17).

Before celebrating the eucharist, Paul wanted the assembled Christians to examine themselves on their relationships with one another. Were they truly members of the Body of Christ sharing a common existence? Did they really belong to one another? Or were they merely in the same space as others, without any bond or exchange of energy? These questions should still be in the mind of every believer who participates in the service of reconciliation that precedes the liturgy of the eucharist in our churches.

PRAYER

Lord, may I not mock you by participating in loveless eucharists where there is no sharing.

IS JESUS TRULY LORD?

THE CORINTHIANS RAISED the topic of spiritual gifts in their letter to Paul (7:1). In other cases of this type, an understanding of the dialogue demanded the reconstruction of the situations that they wanted to bring to Paul's attention. Here we must attempt to do the same.

In chapter 14 it will become clear that Paul had a problem with the importance that some at Corinth gave to the gift of tongues. But was this the only issue? It would be most unusual for Paul to spend two chapters easing slowly into a topic. He does not do so anywhere else in the letter. Moreover, he certainly did not have the sort of legal mind that delights in precise formulation and careful preparation of the ground. He was much more inclined to jump without looking, and he had no compunction about landing on people's toes.

Hence we must assume that the way he *begins* his discussion of spiritual gifts has direct relevance to the situation at Corinth.

Under the Control of the Holy Spirit

THE IDEA THAT the community was a spiritual temple because of the indwelling of the Holy Spirit was fundamental to Paul's theology (3:16; 6:19). From this it was but a short step to seeing the talents of his converts as activities of the Spirit. To insist on this point in his preaching would have been an effective way of reminding them that their lives were lived under the inspiration of grace.

Attractive as it might be, this approach had snags that Paul had not foreseen. Not for the first time, his lack of precision created an opportunity for the Corinthians to misunderstand him. To say that the lives of believers were controlled by the Holy Spirit opened the door for some to justify whatever they did as due to an impulse of the Holy Spirit over which they had no control. For example, a member could disrupt liturgical assemblies by claiming, "The Holy Spirit is irresistibly moving me to say . . ." and go on interminably. Social and liturgical life would quickly become completely chaotic.

The Corinthians could hardly have anticipated Paul's response. He reminded them of what they had experienced before their conversion. This verse (12:2) is the most formal evidence of the religious origins of the majority in the Church at Corinth. They had been devotees of false gods, who were incapable of speech (as of everything else). During the ceremonies honoring such gods the crowds were often swept off their feet by a frenzy of devotion. Carried on a wave of enthusiasm they uttered cries whose incoherence betrayed their otherworldly origin.

Now, of course, the erstwhile pagans in the Church at Corinth realize that all of this was entirely subjective. Idols did not exist and had no power (8:4). The worshipers had deceived themselves. Their "inspiration" had been self-generated. Implicitly Paul invites them to see a parallel with their present conduct in Christian religious assemblies.

The Real Criterion

IF THE IMPULSE of the Holy Spirit is not self-authenticating, there must be an objective criterion by which believers can judge what really comes from the Holy Spirit. For Paul, Jesus is the touchstone of truth.

Anything that affirms the lordship of the historical Jesus necessarily comes from the Holy Spirit. Paul is thinking not only of the verbal confession of faith (Philippians 2:11), but principally of a life lived in imitation of a Lord who, out of love, chose the death of a criminal on the cross. Lordship is best acknowledged by obedience.

On the contrary, anything that smacks of selfishness or affirms the primacy of self in effect denies the significance of Jesus in the lives of believers. To bring out the magnitude of such repudiation Paul formulates it as a curse directed against Jesus. This is perfectly in line with Paul's earlier assertion (11:27) that the behavior of some at the eucharist had identified them as murderers of Christ.

PRAYER
God, let my life proclaim the lordship of Jesus Christ.

A VARIETY OF GIFTS

PAUL BY NOW had learned to read the situation at Corinth. From a few hints he could work out what was going on, even if he sometimes failed to understand why certain people acted as they did. His own experience as a Pharisee (Galatians 1:14) had introduced him to the dynamics of intensely fervent groups. Once aware that spiritual gifts were widespread in the community, he knew that competitiveness would rear its ugly head.

Some would think that certain gifts were superior to others and that they conferred higher status, not only within the community but as a mark of divine favor. Others would feel left out because they were not conscious of having received any special gift. In order to diffuse this situation Paul had to remind the Corinthians of a number of points whose relevance they had not recognized.

The Source of Spiritual Gifts

THE WAY PAUL begins becomes intelligible if we assume that the Corinthians, and possibly Paul himself, spoke indiscriminately of the source of gifts as God, the Lord, and the Holy Spirit. With the propensity of the Corinthians to give the most improbable meaning to anything that Paul said, he had to ensure that this differentiation would not feed the competitive spirit at Corinth.

At first sight he appears to encourage such differentiation by associating "gift" with the Spirit, "service" with the Lord, and "operation" with God. But he immediately makes it clear that it is God who "operates all things in everyone." Thus every "gift" is spiritual and directed to "service," of which the supreme example is the self-sacrificing Lord.

The way Paul speaks here of God, Lord, and Spirit can easily give the impression that he is speaking of the Trinity. The language is certainly capable of bearing that meaning, and such formulations (see 2 Corinthians 13:14) facilitated the later development of Trinitarian theology. For Paul, however, Christ is not "God the Son," nor is the Spirit an independent "person."

Paul did not deny the Trinity. He simply never thought in such terms. Christ was above all the New Adam (15:45), whose perfect humanity illustrated what God intended for his creatures. Subsequently the evangelist John and others would go deeper into the mystery of Christ and recognize divinity.

Similarly Paul saw the Holy Spirit as the activity of God or Christ in history. This is why he speaks indiscriminately of the Spirit of God or the Spirit of Christ (Romans 8:9). Concretely it is the inspiring atmosphere of a genuine Christian community where grace is experienced.

For the Common Good

NO MATTER HOW diverse are the spiritual gifts, they are all directed not to the benefit or gratification of the recipients, but to the common good of the community. Paul does not actually use the term "common good," which can be misleading if it is understood in the same sense as in politics. In a community of action, such as the state, the common good is superior to each individual, who in consequence may be sacrificed for it. For example, it is taken for granted that even the fairest tax system will ruin certain individuals. On the contrary, in a community of being, such as the Church, the common good is identified with the success of each member, which is precisely what Paul wants to bring out by saying that gifts are given "for mutual profit." Only by focusing on the benefit to others can service by Christ-like.

In what forms can the activities of the Spirit become manifest in the community? The possibilities, obviously, are almost infinite. Paul certainly does not intend to limit them by the examples he provides here. Nor does he intend to be exhaustive. Other gifts appear in similar lists elsewhere (12:28–30; Romans 12:6–8). Pentecostal groups have attempted to systematize the gifts and give them very precise definitions. The wide variety in the results confirms that Paul had in mind only very generic types of activity.

PRAYER
God, aid me to recognize my gifts and to use them for mutual benefit.

THE BODY OF CHRIST

PAUL HAS ALREADY spoken of the Body of Christ in 10:16–17 in a way that betrays that he is reminding the Corinthians about something that they should have known. Similarly in 11:29 he takes it for granted that his readers will know what is meant by "discerning the Body." Evidently the topic was one that he had explained in detail during his eighteen-month stay at Corinth during his first visit to the city when he founded the Church (Acts 18:1–18).

Talking About Unity and Multiplicity

THE CORINTHIANS, HOWEVER, had just as much difficulty in grasping what Paul meant as we do today. They had been conditioned to think individualistically, as we have. What strikes us when we regard any Christian community is the diverse multiplicity of the members. Their unity we take on faith. It certainly is not obvious.

This alone shows how far we are from Paul's perspective and what an effort we have to make if we are to understand why he calls the Church the Body of Christ. His statement here is similar to the one he made in 10:17 (which is paralleled by Romans 12:5), "We, who are many, are one body." The statement about unity stands in the principal clause—"we are one body"—as if it were the most obvious thing in the world. The notion of multiplicity appears in the subordinate clause—"who are many"—which carries the connotation "in spite of," as if the multiplicity were somehow doubtful. What was clear to Paul is obscure to us and vice versa. This, of course, means that what he takes for granted we resist. It is up to us to overcome our highly individualistic conditioning.

Why Did Paul Present the Church as a Body?

MANY SCHOLARS BELIEVE that Paul picked up the term "body" from the political writings of his age which often described a city or a political system in terms of a body. This is highly improbable. For Paul the Church was the antithesis of society, and to borrow a term used to characterize the latter in order to describe the former would have been absurd. If, nonetheless, he used the term "body" for the Church, it must have been because he had an overriding reason to do so.

As we shall see in the next chapter, Paul believed that "loving" was the very being of a Christian (13:2). This meant that believers were intimately related in a way that those who lived in an uncaring society were not. To get this across to people who all their lives had taken their individual identity for granted proved extremely difficult. They saw themselves as completely independent. They needed shopkeepers and other services, but in the last analysis they could survive without them. They stood alone. Only a very vivid image had any hope of convincing them that as believers they belonged together, that they were dependent on one another, that they needed each other just to exist.

Paul found this image in the human body. None of its members are alike. The head is completely different from the foot. The hand in no way resembles the ear. Yet they all share a common existence. They belong together, as parts of one being. If that bond is broken, each member is no longer what it was. An amputated arm continues to look like an arm (for a while), but it cannot do any of the things an arm was designed to do. It cannot grip or twist. It is dead.

For Paul those in society were "dead" (Colossians 2:13), isolated from each other in all but the most basic functional terms (see 1:10–17). The function of the Church was to bring them together so that they "belonged" to each other in love. Only then could they come "alive."

PRAYER
Lord, help me to realize that I exist fully only in loving others.

DIVERSITY NECESSARY

THE FACTIOUSNESS OF its members meant that the unity of the community at Corinth was never far from Paul's mind. He availed himself of every opportunity to reinforce the bonds among believers. It is most unlikely that he ever imagined that one could have too much of this particular good thing, but the Corinthians caught him off balance. They all wanted the same spiritual gift. The gift of tongues carried great social prestige, and it was everyone's ambition to possess it.

The Benefits of a Good Education

TARSUS, THE CITY in which Paul spent the first twenty years of his life, had one of the great universities of the ancient world. It did not attract many students from abroad, but it gave its own young men a first-class education which carried them to eminent posts in other countries. It was Paul's academic home for four years in his late teens, and he made the most of it. Only in recent years has it been recognized how well he mastered the techniques of speech-making and letter-writing. He was in his late fifties when he wrote this letter, and his skill had become so polished and habitual that his use of literary techniques appears effortless.

Here he livens up his text by giving speaking roles to different parts of the body. He personifies "the foot" and "the ear," which were chosen because of the similarity of sound of the Greek terms, *pous* and *ous* respectively. These in turn determined the choice of the alternatives. Hand and foot are an obvious pair, as are hearing and seeing.

Paul does not explain why the foot/ear is unhappy because it is not the hand/eye. He may have been influenced by the famous political parable (preserved in both Greek and Latin sources) in which the stomach is envied by all the other members. They had to work, whereas "it had nothing to do but to enjoy the good things which they bestowed upon it" (Livy 2. 32. 9). Paul, however, wanted to mention only the visible parts of the body, because the problem at Corinth concerned public gifts.

There is no logic to the assertion of the foot/ear that it does not belong to the body because it is not another member. The absurdity, of course, is precisely the point that Paul wants to make. And he hammers it home by powerful rhetorical questions.

The Discontent of Some

PAUL'S IMAGE IMPLIES that some members of the community were dissatisfied with the gifts they had received. If they did not have the gift of tongues, they felt that they were nobodies. They were convinced that they made no contribution to the community, and so did not really belong.

Paul's first response to this situation is that saying or thinking something does not make it so. To say that one has a car does not give possession. To say that one does not have a house does not remove the burden of taxes. Similarly those who had been baptized into Christ did not cease to be members of the Body simply by thinking or saying that they had. Those who lacked the gift of tongues were not negligible, and did not make themselves so by saying it.

Paul's second response is that a body is inconceivable without a variety of members. Were a physical body to be reduced to only one of its component parts, such as the nose, it would no longer be what we understand as a body. Similarly, the Body of Christ would no longer exist if all its members possessed the same gift. Furthermore, variety is the very nature of a body, which needs different functions to survive. The foot moves the hand to where it can pick fruit, which is then chewed by the mouth, swallowed by the throat, passed into the stomach, and so sustains the body. Equally, diverse spiritual gifts are necessary to meet the varied requirements of community life. Typically, Paul concludes with an affirmation of unity.

PRAYER
Lord, let me be content with the gifts that have been given me.

NO HIERARCHY IN GIFTS

IF THERE WERE some at Corinth who felt left out because they had not been blessed with a socially esteemed spiritual gift, there were others who had received such a gift and, in consequence, preened themselves on their superiority.

The haves and the have-nots with respect to spiritual gifts agreed on one thing. The gifts were organized in a hierarchy. The envy of the less gifted would not permit them to object to this basic assumption, which was enthusiastically supported by the favored ones. It put them at the top of the ladder. They not only looked down on all others, which was bad enough in Christian terms, but dismissed them as irrelevant, which was much more serious. One cannot write off people and still claim to love them.

The divisions arising out of the assumption that the gifts were arranged in a hierarchy forced Paul to question its validity.

What Is Indispensable?

ONCE AGAIN PAUL gives a voice to parts of the body. Those chosen are easily seen as superior. The eye directs the hand, and the head is carried by the feet. The eye, however, dismisses the hand, and the head proclaims the irrelevance of the feet. As in the previous section, simply to articulate the idea reveals its absurdity.

The ancient parable of the privileged stomach makes the point beautifully. "The members conspired together, that the hands should carry no food to the mouth, nor the mouth accept anything that was given it, nor the teeth grind up what they received. While they sought in this angry spirit to starve the belly into submission, the members themselves and the whole body were reduced to the utmost weakness" (Livy, 2. 32. 10). Thus the other members were forced to recognize that the stomach made a crucial contribution.

This is precisely what Paul means when he says that "the parts of the body which seem to be weaker are indispensable" (11:22). Implicitly he contrasts weaker and stronger, when he really means internal and external. The contrast is between the obvious parts of the body, such as the head and eyes, and the internal organs. Just because the heart, liver, kidneys, and so on cannot be seen does not mean that they can be dismissed as irrelevant. Our knowledge of medicine makes us much more aware than Paul could ever have been of the indispensable contributions that such organs make, but the parable quoted above reveals that his generation knew something of the importance of the invisible parts of the body.

The Principle of Compensation

FOR THOSE WHO might not have understood his rather subtle argument based on the contrast between the internal and external parts of the body, Paul provides a further argument that all can understand. The wordplay in Greek is brilliant, but unfortunately untranslatable.

From one point of view the sexual organs are considered disgraceful. They are not exposed to public view. Yet at the same time great attention is devoted to them, and they are clothed with great care. In other words, appearances are deceptive, and the Corinthians should beware of those gifts which attract the most prestige.

Unity in Diversity

ONCE AGAIN PAUL concludes by emphasizing the unity of the community. He uses the body image in a most effective way to remind the believers of their intimate involvement with each other. When a person has a toothache all the members of the body are distracted, just as all luxuriate when the back is given a good massage. Were the community genuinely the Body of Christ, all believers would suffer when one was injured, and all would glow with happiness when one was honored.

Having argued consistently and effectively against a hierarchy in the spiritual gifts, Paul appears to wreck his achievement at the very end by listing three ministries as first, second, and third. The ranking, however, is chronological. Apostles establish churches, prophets provide stimulus to new converts, and teachers pass on the traditions as the community stabilizes.

PRAYER
God, make me remember that spiritual gifts are for service,
not satisfaction.

LOVING IS BEING

THE TRADITION OF classical rhetoric, in which Paul was trained, advised a "digression" in the course of a complex development. It was a trick to win the goodwill of the audience by giving them a momentary break from the concentration needed to follow an argument. It was also a moment when the speaker/writer was encouraged to give his talent full rein in order to delight and relax his audience. The only condition was that there had to be some connection with the matter under discussion.

What Paul does in this celebrated "Hymn to Love" perfectly illustrates not only his knowledge of the rules of rhetoric, but the perfection of his technique. Although there are subtle links to the spiritual gifts, the topic is different, and his language soars rhythmically. He shifts our perspective to a fundamental theme that underlies the whole thrust of this letter.

Gifts Without Love

THE DIGRESSION OPENS with three statements all constructed on the same pattern: "If I have . . . but have not love, I am . . ." The abrupt shift to the first person singular reinforces the dramatic rhythm of the repetition. No one hearing the letter read aloud could be unaware that something new was going on, even if the reader was not very good. Yet there are echoes of what Paul has just been speaking about in that love is contrasted with spiritual gifts.

The fact that Paul mentions first "the tongues of men and of angels" indicates once again that the gift of speaking in tongues is at the top of his agenda in this part of the letter. The natural sense of "tongues of men" is foreign languages (Paul's education would have made him familiar with Hebrew, Aramaic, and Greek); but "tongues of angels" can only be speech that is unintelligible to humans. When pronounced without care for others, it resembles "sounding brass." Stone theaters did not enhance the actors' voices by resonance, as the older wooden theaters had done. To compensate, brass vases were located at strategic points. They were turned upside down and tilted open toward the stage by wedges. When tuned, they contributed a resonant hum that gave body to the actors' voices, but was in itself unintelligible.

The other spiritual gifts evoked by Paul are prophecy, knowledge, and faith, all of which appear in 12:8–10. The relation of faith to moving mountains reflects Paul's knowledge of the teaching of Jesus: "If you have faith as a grain of mustard seed, you will say to this mountain, 'Move hence to yonder place,' and it will move" (Matthew 17:20; Mark 11:23).

The gift of "helping" (12:28) is dramatized in rendering oneself destitute in order to help another, and in the acceptance of a supremely painful death in a great cause. Yet both are barren gestures if they are not inspired by love.

Without Love I Am Nothing

THE MOST FUNDAMENTAL statement in this opening section of the "Hymn to Love" is "Without love I am nothing" (13:2). This should not be read as if it were the equivalent of "I am useless." Paul means that without love we do not exist. In other words, we come into being through loving. Paul here diverges radically from every philosophical view of human nature. He took seriously the revelation of Christ. In giving himself for us, Christ revealed that true humanity consisted in loving (Galatians 2:20). Loving is what makes a person genuinely human.

Love, however, must have as its object another person. Thus, A exists as human and as Christian only in loving B. One cannot be a completely isolated Christian. There must always be an active reference to at least one other person. Here we find the profound reason why Paul had to think of the Church in terms of an organic unity such as the human body. The lover and the beloved share a common existence in precisely the same way as the arm and the leg coexist.

PRAYER
Lord, give me the gift of loving.

WHAT IS LOVE?

EVERY GENERATION BEMOANS the passing of the good old days. This has been true since the beginning of time. In the first century A.D., Quintilian, the famous teacher of rhetoric, complained about the destructive influence of first-class secretaries. Their ability to take dictation at the speed of normal speech intimidated their masters with the result that "in our desire to produce a continuous flow, we become positively sloppy" (*Institutio Oratoria*, 10. 3. 20).

Quality Writing

PAUL, WE KNOW, used professional secretaries, because one of them added a personal note at the end of the letter to the Romans, presumably because there was space left over: "I Tertius, the writer of this letter, greet you in the Lord" (16:22). Were the awkward hanging phrases that occur in Paul's letters due to the pressure to keep going generated by a highly competent secretary? We don't know. Yet Paul (perhaps when he went at his own speed) could write beautiful tightly focused prose. The lyrical expression of what love does and does not do is a case in point. It is intimately related to the situation at Corinth while at the same time transcending it. It has both universal appeal and specific relevance. We can detect the faults of the Corinthians and the virtues they neglected.

The diverse aspects of love are expressed both positively and negatively. Paul affirms two positive qualities, denies eight negative qualities, and returns to five positive qualities.

What Love Does

JUST HOW FUNDAMENTAL "patience" and "kindness" are emerges from the fact that they are characteristics of God (Romans 2:4) and the fruit of the Spirit (Galatians 5:22), which are manifested in Paul's own ministry (2 Corinthians 6:6). Love puts up with everything, while reaching out with gentleness. Precisely these qualities were lacking in the way the Strong treated the scruples of the Weak in regard to the eating of idol meat (chapter 8).

Paul virtually repeats himself in saying that love "supports" and "endures" everything (13:7). There could hardly be a better description of his own attitude toward the Corinthians. He had to take a lot from them, and at times his patience was stretched very thin, but he never gave up. If they spoke, he would respond. No matter how far they tried him, he would never lose "faith" in them. Nor would he ever cease to "hope" that they would grow into mature Christians. Paul's love is tenacious and optimistic, like all true love that does not alter "when it alteration finds" (Shakespeare).

What Love Does Not Do

CERTAIN PEOPLE AT Corinth were "jealous" of the spiritual gifts enjoyed by others who, no doubt, "boasted" of their superiority. Those who attached themselves to different leaders within the Church believed that their factions were the best. Their "pride" was misplaced.

"Unseemly behavior" in the liturgical assemblies had been the target of Paul's ire on several occasions. Long hair on men and carelessly arranged hair on women was unseemly in terms of the cultural conventions of the first century. The gluttony and drunkenness of the wealthier members of the community at the eucharist was unseemly in a much more radical sense.

"Self-seeking" was manifest in the attitudes of both Weak and Strong with respect to eating idol meat. Each side was so focused on its own needs that the other was vilified as stupid or hypocritical, respectively. Paul had to tell them explicitly, "Let no one seek his own good, but the good of the other" (10:24). He never considered his own advantage (10:33).

Paul did not "keep a record of wrongs" of the Corinthians. Once each problem had been worked out, the slate was wiped clean. There were so many problems, however, that he was often "irritated" at the Corinthians' childishness. He was aware of his failings, and struggled to overcome them. His love did not strive to find fault. He preferred to rejoice in what he saw was solid and true.

PRAYER
Lord, let my love be true.

GROWING UP

THE POWER OF Paul's writing in this "Hymn to Love" has been noted several times in the two previous sections. The concluding part exhibits the same qualities. Paul often organizes his material in an A-B-A pattern, veering away from a subject only to return to it from another angle—for example, sex–lawsuits–sex in chapters 5–6. The same phenomenon occurs here. The first verses in this section pick up the spiritual gifts of "prophecy," "tongues," and "knowledge," which had been mentioned in the opening verses of the hymn.

"Now" and "Then"

OUR APPRECIATION OF Paul's literary skill becomes more marked when we observe the clever construction of this paragraph. Verse 8 mentions three gifts, "prophecy," "tongues," and "knowledge." These are reduced to two, "knowledge" and "prophecy," in the following verse. And finally in verse 12 we are left with "knowledge" alone. The tightening focus highlights "knowledge" as the issue.

With what is this "knowledge" concerned? Traditionally it has been thought to be God. This inference is based on the imperfection of our present "knowledge," which is described as "seeing in a mirror dimly," and its perfection in the future when we "shall see face to face." The contrast, apparently, is between our indirect knowledge of God in this life and the clarity of the beatific vision in heaven.

Paul is certainly thinking in terms of "now" and "then," but the last verse makes it most improbable that by "then" he means the next life. How can "faith" remain when full vision has been achieved? (See 2 Corinthians 5:7.) How can "hope" remain when the desired object has been obtained? (See Romans 8:24.) Moreover, Jacob saw God "face to face" (Genesis 32:30), as did Moses (Exodus 33:11; Numbers 12:8), and no one ever thought that they had been transferred to heaven. The phrase "face to face" denotes only the openness of genuine communication, not the sphere in which it takes place.

From Childishness to Maturity

IF "NOW" AND "then" do not evoke earthly and heavenly lives, they can only refer to two phases of the present lives of the Corinthians. What they are is contrasted with what they can and must become.

To soften what he is going to say, and to demonstrate the leadership by example on which he has insisted (11:1), Paul speaks of what has happened in his life. Once he exhibited the behavioral patterns of a child, but these were not maintained into adulthood. They were inappropriate to his new status as a mature individual.

The relevance to the situation of the Corinthians becomes clear when we remember that Paul had already told them, "I could not address you as spiritual people, but as fleshly people, as babes in Christ" (3:1). In the next chapter he will exhort them, "Do not be infantile in your thinking. Be babes in evil, but in thinking be mature" (14:20).

The need for such a warning is evident. We have noted a number of cases where the behavior of the Corinthians, who flattered themselves on their intellectual sophistication, could only be characterized as childish, notably their blurring of the distinction between the sexes in order to fulfill Paul's assertion that there was no more male and female (Galatians 3:28).

By implication Paul is telling them here that the importance they attach to spiritual gifts is misplaced. Such gifts do not have a permanent value. They are not in the same league as faith, hope, and charity, which will always be essential ingredients of the Christian life. The gifts are a temporary aid designed to give the new Christian movement a good start. The task of a booster rocket is finished once the space vehicle is well launched on its flight.

The permanent force that binds a community together and propels it into mission is love, which is the flower of faith and the ground of hope.

PRAYER
Lord, help me to distinguish in the Church between the essential and the superficial, between the permanent and the transitory.

PROPHECY CLOSEST TO LOVE

WERE PAUL UNDER no restrictions, he would have insisted that faith working through love was the only essential element in the Christian life. His view of the community as the place where the Spirit of God was present, however, left him no option but to recognize that certain Christian activities were manifestations of the Spirit. He could not repudiate them. All he could do was attempt to educate the Corinthians to a healthier attitude toward the gifts.

Speaking in Tongues

WE HAVE NO direct evidence that the Corinthians attached great importance to the gift of tongues. It is a deduction from Paul's response. It would have been pointless for him to spend so much time and effort on a gift which he considered socially irrelevant, unless it had been given undue significance at Corinth. What precisely did the gift of tongues involve?

Any answer to this question is complicated by the broad range of opinions generated by the proliferation of the phenomenon in the twentieth-century charismatic movement. Here we must focus on what Paul tells us, and the crucial verse is 14:5, which reads, "He who prophesies is greater than he who speaks in tongues unless the latter can interpret what they say so the Church is built up by it." This clearly identifies two stages in the gift, the first characterized by unintelligible sounds, and the second by words understood by all.

All the Pauline allusions to tongues fall into place if we envisage the initial babbling stage as one in which a believer cannot find the words to express an intense religious emotion. He or she feels that they have been touched by the Spirit, and must tell the assembly. The experience, however, is so ineffable that the intellect cannot grasp it completely. Inevitably the mind cannot find words. All that emerges are incoherent sounds. They betray the presence of the Spirit, but in a secret way that the Corinthians felt enhanced the standing of the one so blessed. He or she was set aside from others and in direct communion with God.

Paul pours cold water on such enthusiasm for the mysterious. Such persons should refrain from trying to speak until they calm down and can find the words to make their experience meaningful to others.

Prophecy

PAUL, IT WILL be noticed, does not deny the authenticity of the religious experience of the babbler. He has no interest in the gift in itself, but only in its relation to the community. All gifts are for the common good, not for the gratification of the recipient (12:7). Thus Paul gives pride of place to the gift that makes the greatest contribution to the development of the community, namely, prophecy.

In Paul's world, "prophet" had a wide range of meanings both religious and secular, ranging from the highest mystic authority to the announcer at sports meetings. There is wide agreement among scholars that in the early Church the Christian prophet was "an immediately inspired spokesperson for God, the risen Jesus, or the Spirit who received intelligible oracles that he or she felt impelled to deliver to the Christian community or, representing the community, to the general public" (*Anchor Bible Dictionary*, 5:496).

While this definition should be kept in mind in the sections that follow, Paul's concern here is with the impact of such oracles on the Church. He singles out three areas, which make it clear that he is not thinking in terms of predictions of the future. "Upbuilding" is the most basic. The term returns repeatedly. It is the work of "love" in 8:1, and covers every positive contribution to the community. "Encouragement" was necessary to preserve the fervor of those who had left their familiar world to become Christians. They also needed "comfort," not in the weak sense of tender loving care, but in the strong sense of "strength-giving." To give in these ways is authentic leadership, a role exercised by both men and women at Corinth (11:4–5).

PRAYER

God, grant that I may contribute to the growth of my local church.

NO MEANING, NO ACTION

HAVING EXPLAINED WHY speaking in tongues is inferior to prophecy, Paul heaps up arguments to put tongues in their proper place.

A Babbling Apostle

THE CORINTHIANS CONSIDERED speaking in tongues to be a sign of superior spirituality. The mysterious noises betrayed the takeover of the personality by the Spirit. Those standing by felt themselves to be in the presence of the numinous. Paul's reaction is, "What then?"

To make the point that something more is necessary if a gift is to be profitable to the community, Paul asks his audience to run through a little scenario in their imaginations. What would have happened had he arrived in Corinth speaking in tongues?

Would anyone who heard him have identified these sounds as evidence of the presence of the Spirit of God? It is much more likely that they would have been dismissed as fake religious ecstasy. In that case Paul would have been classed as one of the unscrupulous charlatans who traveled the country making a good living out of the credulous.

Suppose, nonetheless, that some kind soul took pity on Paul and offered him hospitality, how could he learn anything of the gospel unless Paul spoke intelligibly? Had Paul spoken only in tongues, the Corinthians would never have heard of Jesus Christ.

Even if Paul came to Corinth now and spoke only in tongues, it would not profit the Corinthians. They already knew that he was gifted with the power of the Spirit; the existence of the Church proved that (9:2). Would they really be satisfied by a visit during which he made only unintelligible sounds? Such evidence of his superior spirituality would surely pall after a day or so.

A new religious insight, on the contrary, would enrich their lives. It might come in the form of "revelation," "knowledge," "prophecy," or "teaching." Many have attempted to define these spiritual gifts in such a way that they are adequately distinguished from one another, but there is no guarantee that Paul thought in such mutually exclusive categories. Why should not a "teaching" communicate revealed knowledge? At this point he is interested only in what all these gifts have in common. They convey something intelligible to the mind of the hearer.

Musical Instruments

FROM THE PERSONAL, Paul now turns to analogies drawn from musical instruments. The indispensable role of music in human life is underlined by the fact that Genesis 4:17–22 lists "Jubal, the ancestor of all who play the harp and the pipe" among the "first" city planner, the "first" herdsman, and the "first" blacksmith.

It is perhaps just a coincidence that Paul mentions the same types of instruments as does Genesis—one that produces music by having its strings plucked and the other by the vibration of air forced into it. The only other category of ancient instruments, those of resonant material that make sounds when shaken or struck (drum, rattle, cymbal), would have been inappropriate for Paul's purpose because they cannot carry a tune.

Hearing someone speak in tongues, Paul says, is like listening idly to a flutist or a harpist playing random notes in order to get his or her instrument warmed up and in tune. No one really pays attention because the noises are just a preliminary to real music. Similarly, tentative notes on a trumpet produce no effect. The sounding of the agreed summons to battle is a different matter.

Why should the Corinthians think that speaking in tongues is any different from these common-sense examples whose truth they would be the first to recognize? Unintelligible speech is like the wind, which makes all sorts of noises but says nothing.

Finally Paul returns to his own experience. In a cosmopolitan city like Corinth he had met many foreigners whose language he could not understand. He could see in their eyes the frustration of the effort to communicate, but they could not get through to him. He learned nothing from them. He did not profit in any way. It was as if they spoke in tongues.

PRAYER
Lord, help me to speak and act in such a way that others will truly
understand me.

PRAY TO BE UNDERSTOOD

PAUL HAS MADE it abundantly clear that speaking in tongues is babbling. Now he takes up the problem of the impact of such meaningless speech on the community. The underlying principle is that the goal of corporate worship is not a personal thrill but the building up of the Body of Christ.

Try Harder

PAUL WAS AN astute judge of human nature. He was fully aware that the prestige associated with speaking in tongues would tend to make those who had received the gift reluctant to move from this initial stage of religious insight. Once they had calmed down, and reflected, they should be capable of saying what they had experienced. Then, however, they would drop a number of places on the ladder of socioreligious status because their speech was intelligible and thus similar to many other gifts.

Hence, Paul says, those who are gifted with unformed and vague, but nonetheless genuine, religious insights should pray that God may bring them the step further which will enable them to speak plainly. Just below the surface of the text is the unspoken insinuation that those who remain at the tongues stage are somehow stunted in their spiritual development.

By noting that the mind in the case of speaking in tongues is "unfruitful," Paul plants a further delicate barb. It was designed to hit a sensitive spot among the intellectuals at Corinth who prided themselves on the power and sophistication of their intellects. They prized the mind except in the one instance where unintelligibility gave them social prominence! Not very consistent, murmurs Paul.

Community Approbation

DESPITE PAUL'S ESTIMATE of speaking in tongues as inferior to prophecy, he never denies the validity of the theological insight that is struggling for expression. On the contrary, if it is truly from the Holy Spirit it has a value for the community. The community, however, cannot benefit unless it understands what is being said.

Paul took it for granted that the presence of the Holy Spirit meant that all the members of the Church had something to contribute. Each member brought to the assembly "a hymn, a lesson, a revelation" (14:26). Paul here speaks of singing with mind and spirit, and elsewhere mentions "psalms, and hymns, and spiritual songs" (Colossians 3:16), which may be illustrated by the profound Christological hymns that he quotes in Philippians 2:6–11 and Colossians 1:15–20.

Early theological development took place by means of such quantum leaps of faith. They had to pass a test, however, before being incorporated into the creed of the community. They had to be coherent with the core of what was already accepted. Such consistency was recognized by the community shouting "Amen," a term borrowed from Hebrew and meaning "this is true and valid." An utterance greeted by silence slipped from the consciousness of the Church, never to be heard of again.

Boasting

IT IS EASY to imagine the surprise with which the Corinthians heard Paul say "I speak in tongues more than you all" (14:18). Why would he boast of something against which he had spoken so strongly when the gift came to the Corinthians? We must remember, however, that what Paul criticized was the public manifestation of the gift. He had conceded that speaking in tongues is to utter "mysteries in the Spirit" (14:2) which edifies the speaker (14:4). One has the clear impression that Paul would have had no objection to the gift were it exercised in private.

PRAYER
God, help me to contribute to the theological development of my local community.

THE MISSIONARY ASPECT

A NOTE OF extreme exasperation is easily detected in the opening words, "It is okay to be childlike in your freedom from malice, but for heaven's sake try to think like adults. Grow up!" Like children attracted by the gaudy, the Corinthians preferred the flashy gift of tongues. They should have been more perceptive, particularly in view of the missionary function of the church.

A Prophetic Text

THE RELEVANCE OF Paul's quotation of Isaiah 28:11–12 to the condition of the Church at Corinth becomes clear only when we recall the situation against which Isaiah is reacting (28:7ff.). Once again Paul presumes a rather detailed knowledge of the scriptures on the part of his audience.

Priests and prophets taking part in a drunken orgy in the temple dismiss the warnings of Isaiah as words without meaning: "Whom does he think he is lecturing . . . with his 'Sav lasav, sav lasav, kav lakav, kav lakav, zeer sham, zeer sham'" (28:10). The resemblance to speaking in tongues is inescapable, but the spirit behind this babbling was alcohol! Then God pronounces the words that Paul cites, and continues with the same nonsense syllables, which imply that the people will be "broken, trapped, and taken captive" (28:13). The context, therefore, makes it clear that the "other tongues on the lips of foreigners" are the languages of an invading army. Such gibberish is a sign of the divine punishment that will fall on the Israelites.

From this episode Paul draws a conclusion that causes problems only if one accepts the misleading translation of 14:22 in all modern versions. What he actually says is, "Tongues are a sign, not for the faithful, but for the unfaithful." He is thinking in terms of behavior, not of belief. In the perspective of the event recorded by Isaiah the presence of tongues in the community should be taken as a warning, not as a blessing. Its message is that the conduct of the Corinthians is not acceptable to God. The importance they gave to speaking in tongues was but another example of the selfishness that characterized much of their relations with one another.

Prophecy, on the contrary, is a sign to the "faithful," those who loyally maintain their commitment to Christ, because the gift stimulates their service to each other. Its call to selflessness is nonsense to the "unfaithful." These are not only outsiders but, above all, Christians in name only.

Unexpected Visitors

PLEASING AS THE scriptural paradox was in perplexing the Corinthians, Paul had to ensure that they got the point that speaking in tongues injured the mission of the Church to outsiders. He invites them to contemplate two scenarios.

In the first scenario, nonbelievers stray into an assembly of Christians where everyone is speaking in tongues. They see a group of individuals mouthing meaningless words without the slightest concern for one another. "They must all be raving maniacs" is the only conclusion the visitors could reach. Whatever interest they might have felt in Christianity is stifled. The behavior of the Corinthians obliterated the distinctive identity of Christianity. It was made to appear one of the many pagan cults whose adherents were maddened by the inspiration of the god.

A very different impression would be made on casual visitors if, according to the second scenario, all the members of the church prophesy. The concern for one another expressed in edification, encouragement, and consolation (14:3) is so obviously good, and so evidently at variance with the self-centeredness of society, that it forces the visitors to look at their own lives. The contrast obliges them to recognize the obstacles that society puts in the way of their giving the best of themselves. They can see that in a loving community it would be easy to be good and true. They see the power of God at work, and confess his presence in the Church.

PRAYER
Lord, help me to remember that all that I am should proclaim the presence of grace in my life.

NOT TOO LONG

FROM ALL THAT Paul says it is certain that the Corinthians were plentifully blessed with gifts of the Holy Spirit. Unfortunately this went hand in hand with a lamentable lack of judgment, for example their preference for the socially prestigious gift of tongues rather than the infinitely more useful gift of prophecy. Not surprisingly, their liturgical assemblies were chaotic. Each had something to say. Each claimed priority in the name of the Holy Spirit. The result? Everyone spoke at the same time!

Such meetings would alienate outsiders as effectively as if everyone spoke in tongues (14:23). They also proved extremely stressful for the members of the community. No doubt the gifts that prevailed belonged to those with the biggest voices and the strongest elbows. The rising frustration among those who failed to get a hearing could not fail to have a most destructive effect on the web of loving relations that was the distinctive feature of the Church.

The Need for Common Sense

THE DETRIMENTAL CONSEQUENCES of such chaos clearly showed that it was not intended by God. The action of the Spirit was to promote good. It could not bring about evil. If the spiritual gifts were to benefit the community there had to be order. Paul raises such simple common sense, which the "wise" at Corinth completely failed to grasp, to the level of a theological principle: "God is not a God of disorder but of peace, as in all the churches of the saints" (14:33).

This principle gently reminds the Corinthians, who tended to think of themselves as unique, that they are not the only Christians in the world (1:2). Other communities are also endowed with gifts of the Spirit but conduct themselves in a very different fashion. They are havens of peace in which the interchange of love enables all to follow Christ in tranquillity. If, however, the Corinthians cannot learn from their neighbors, Paul will have to advise them.

Speakers in Tongues

TODAY, AS AT all times, there are those who equate length with solemnity. A religious ceremony, they believe, cannot be short. It must take a long time. Brevity is the equivalent of haste, which is detrimental to dignity. Paul, however, knew—presumably from personal experience—that liturgical assemblies that ran on too long did not have a positive effect on the community. Nothing is more frustrating than a service that does not move steadily forward so that one can foresee that it will end at a reasonable time.

One danger of a ceremony running over time at Corinth came from the speakers in tongues, who were convinced that they had no control over their gift. Paul's sense of the common good convinced him otherwise. "If anyone speaks in a tongue—two or at the most three, and in turn—let that person put his or her insight into words, but if the words won't come, let that person remain silent in the assembly and speak to him/herself and to God" (14:27–28). In other words, there must be no meaningless babble. And those who can verbalize their theological insights must be strictly limited in number at any given meeting.

Prophets

EQUALLY, THE NUMBER of prophets who spoke had to be restricted. These two were not the only gifts (12:8–10, 28), and others had to be given an opportunity to benefit the church. Paul suggests that two or three prophecies would be adequate.

He also stresses that what is revealed in prophecy is not of itself guaranteed (14:16). The community must judge whether it conforms to "the analogy of faith" (Romans 12:6); that is, it must be consistent with what is already believed. Paul's belief in rationality and its role in revelation is underlined by his demand that a prophet should have the humility and generosity to cede the floor if another claims to have received a revelation.

PRAYER
Lord, preserve me from church services that go on and on and on.

AN ATTACK ON WOMEN

SOME WOULD SAY that these verses show that Paul was "antifeminist," and reinforce their conviction that the patriarchal bias of the Church is irreformable. It is my opinion, however, that Paul did not write these verses. Moreover, when put in their proper context they give no support to the patriarchal perspective of some Christians.

Did Paul Write These Words?

THE FIRST ARGUMENT against Pauline authorship of 14:34–35 is the blatant contradiction between these verses and 11:5. In this latter text, as we have seen, Paul takes it for granted that women play a leadership role in prayer and prophecy in the public assemblies of the Church at Corinth. In other words, they do precisely what is forbidden here!

Since it is extremely improbable that Paul contradicted himself, we must assume either that he did not write one of the two passages or that he is not talking about the same thing in both places. One scholar, for example, suggested that in 11:5 Paul is speaking of single women, whereas in 14:34–35 he is thinking of married women. This distinction is anachronistic. In antiquity no daughter (and every single woman was someone's daughter) could be accorded a freedom denied to her mother. If single women were permitted to exercise authority in the Christian community, so were married women. Leadership roles were open to women as such.

This line of argument, which draws attention to the un-Pauline character of 14:34–35, is confirmed by the insistence of these verses that the subordination of women is demanded by the Law. The reference is to Genesis 2:18–23, which deduced the inferiority of woman from the fact that she was created in second place. Paul, however, has repudiated this interpretation in 11:11–12. Moreover, he never appeals to the Law for support in a disciplinary matter. In fact we have seen that he refuses to impose a moral decision on the Corinthians (5:1–5).

It is most improbable, therefore, that Paul penned 14:34–35. Sometime after his death these lines were scribbled in the margin of a copy of this letter. Subsequent copyists thought that their predecessor had made an accidental omission which he had immediately corrected, and they wrote it as part of the letter. One put it here, the other after 14:40.

A Reaction to Pauline Liberalism

THE SOURCE OF 14:34–35 is revealed by 1 Timothy; "I permit no woman to teach or to have authority over men. She is to keep silent. For Adam was formed first, then Eve; and Adam was not deceived, but the woman was deceived" (2:12–14).

This letter cannot have been written by Paul, for whom Adam was the transgressor par excellence (Romans 5:12–21; 1 Corinthians 15:21–22), and Eve the prototype of the entire Corinthian community and not merely of the female element (2 Corinthians 11:3). It stems from a generation after Paul which reacted against many of his policies. For certain Christians, his churches were too far out of step with contemporary society, notably with regard to the freedoms they accorded to women as a right, not a privilege. These churches, some believed, would have a greater impact on pagan society if they were better integrated; in other words, if they conformed to the standards of the world.

A Canonical Problem

THE NEW TESTAMENT, therefore, contains two contradictory statements about the position of women in the Church, one permitting leadership roles and one refusing such activities. Both belong to canonical scripture, but both cannot be lived simultaneously. In practice a choice must be made. One inspired text must be accepted and the other rejected.

The choice is too fundamental to be based on unthinking personal preference. The critical question is: Which text reflects the newness of the gospel and which parrots the values of the world? Without any doubt, 14:34–35 and 1 Timothy 2:12–13 articulate the patriarchalism of a fallen humanity. The freedom of 11:5 is that of the childen of God, the fruit of the gospel.

PRAYER
God, help those opposed to the ordination of women to read
the scriptures honestly.

LAST WORDS

PAUL'S CONCLUDING REMARKS on the use of spiritual gifts by the Corinthians betray the struggle going on inside him. Their persistent refusal to see what he considered obvious generated intense exasperation, which he does not quite succeed in holding in check. There was not much time left (7:29), and it was being frittered away on peripheral matters, which hindered not only the progress of individuals but the apostolic mission of the Church.

A Sharp Reproof

A NUMBER OF scholars do not accept that 14:34–35 is an addition made to this letter after Paul's death. Neither, however, do they believe that it represents Paul's views on the position of women in the Church. They claim that it comes from the letter sent to Paul by the Corinthians (7:1), and that Paul quotes it only in order to refute it.

There is no difficulty in the postulate of a Corinthian quotation. We have seen a number of such quotations, notably in 6:12–20 and 8:1–13, which we were able to print out as a script for a play. Such dialogue, however, shows that Paul reacted to issues raised by the Corinthians by careful consideration and detailed argumentation. If they recognized something as a problem, he was prepared to go to any lengths to help them work through to a genuinely Christian solution. He tended to explode only when he saw a problem where they found none.

Passionately barbed rhetorical questions, such as we have here in verse 36, occur for example in his reaction to divisions within the community (1:13), the case of incest (5:2), and selfishness at the eucharistic assembly (11:22), none of which posed any problem for the Corinthians. Verse 36, therefore, is much less likely to be a response to a Corinthian quotation than a vigorous continuation of Paul's effort to induce order in a charismatic assembly whose riotous character did not bother the Corinthians (11:26–33). Paul's frustration is manifest in the put-down, "Are you the only Christians in the world?" The wounding sarcasm that inspired 4:8–10 surfaces again.

Spiritual People Should Recognize Spiritual Authority

THE CORINTHIANS PRIDED themselves on their possession of "wisdom" and on the profusion of spiritual gifts with which their Church was endowed. As far as Paul was concerned, their "wisdom" was spurious (2:6–16), and he found it impossible to accept many of their attitudes toward spiritual gifts. But in order to turn the tables on them he was prepared to accept their self-evaluation at face value. It gave him the opportunity to force them to draw the conclusion that he wanted. Anger had not blunted his wits!

If the Corinthians are what they claim to be, they are the experts at recognizing what comes from the Holy Spirit. They should be the first, therefore, to acknowledge that Paul acts with the authority of the Lord. Some manuscripts of 14:37 mention "a command of the Lord," but this is almost certainly a deliberate attempt to reinforce the prohibition against the ministry of women in 14:34–35. It is lacking in the same manuscripts that place 14:34–35 *after* 14:40. What Paul means is clear from assertions that he has made earlier in the letter. He claimed to have "the mind of Christ" (2:16) and to "imitate Christ" (11:1) in all things. Paul has so identified with Christ that he can say what the Lord would say were he still on earth and confronted with the problem with which Paul has to deal. Such confidence borders on arrogance, but if Paul did not accept the responsibility of speaking for Christ, who would?

All of a sudden Paul tires of the debate. If anyone does not get the point that he has been struggling to make in so many different ways (10:24), then that person will just have to stay ignorant, with unfortunate consequences when it comes to the moment of divine judgment.

PRAYER
God grant that I may recognize genuine spiritual authority and permit myself to be challenged in my most cherished attitudes.

RESURRECTION VERSUS IMMORTALITY

IT IS ONLY when we get some way into this chapter that we find out that some at Corinth denied the resurrection (15:12). We do not know whether the Corinthians mentioned the problem in their letter (7:1) or whether Paul heard about it from the accompanying delegation (16:17). It is perhaps more probable that Paul deduced that such a denial would surface at Corinth from what he knew of the attitude of some people there toward the body. If, as they believed, the body was entirely irrelevant here on earth (6:18), what role could it possibly play in the next life?

For this chapter to make full sense we need to understand what Paul's contemporaries believed about life after death.

Resurrection from the Dead

THE FIRST PART of the second century B.C. was a watershed in Jewish thinking about survival after death. Prior to that date, death was understood as punishment for sin (Genesis 3:2–3; Sirach 25:24; Wisdom 2:23–24). Even though everyone died at some time or other, it was taken completely for granted that the people as such would survive, and resurrection language, such as occurs in Hosea 6:1–3 and Ezekiel 37:1–14, was used to express the conviction of a national revival.

The Maccabean rebellion against Syria changed all that. For the first time in history Jews were giving their lives in defense of God's law. They were dying because they were obedient to a covenant that promised life. Hence, they concluded, God had to bring them back to life as individuals. This breakthrough is attested to in Daniel 12:1–3, and particularly in 2 Maccabees: "The king of the world will raise us up, since we die for his laws, to live again forever" (7:9).

The verb "to raise up" is used because at this stage Jews believed that the human person was not two things but one, "an animated body" or "an embodied soul." In consequence, the physical body was as indispensable to survival as the spiritual soul, both here and in the next life. They could be thought of as independent, but one could not really exist without the other.

Immortality of the Soul

THE GREEKS HAD a different way of looking at humanity. They thought of the human person as made up of two parts of unequal value. The most important component was the soul, whose entirely spiritual character made it invulnerable to destruction. It was immortal, designed for eternity. In this present life, the soul was imprisoned in a physical body. Not only was the body material and perishable; its needs and desires distracted the soul from its essential functions of contemplating the beautiful and the true. In the Greek perspective the two components of the person were not only distinguishable, they were separable. Even if the body died, the soul continued to exist unchanged. Not only that, the situation of the soul improved. It was no longer dragged down by the passions of the body. It was finally free, forever.

Certain groups in Judaism took over this way of looking at human nature, but with one important modification. They denied that the soul was immortal of itself. The ability of the soul to live forever was given to it by the possession of "wisdom." "In kinship with wisdom there is immortality . . . and I went about seeking her for myself . . . but I perceived that I would not possess wisdom unless God gave her to me" (Wisdom 8:17–21).

A Choice

AT THE TIME of Paul, therefore, one could think of survival after death in two radically different ways. One involved the restoration of a body, whereas the other did not. Those at Corinth who were convinced that they possessed "wisdom" and who disparaged the body would naturally be attracted by the immortality-of-the-soul option. In addition it was the currently fashionable theory. For Paul, however, the only *guaranteed* option was resurrection of the body, because one man had *already* risen from the dead.

PRAYER
God grant that I may be attracted by the real and not by the merely fashionable.

THE CREED

PAUL HERE INVITES the community to recall the precise words (15:2) in which he preached the death and resurrection of Christ, which is the core of the gospel. This will be the basis of a simple two-pronged argument in the paragraphs which follow. If the Corinthians maintain their acceptance of this formula, they cannot avoid its consequences. If they repudiate the formula, they are no longer Christians with all that implies—namely, no Lord of Glory, no "wisdom," no gifts of the Holy Spirit!

A Traditional Formula

THE INTRODUCTION TO the formula is similar to the way Paul presented the eucharistic words (11:23). What follows is not his creation. He is but one link in a chain, handing on unchanged what he himself received. The perfect balance, which facilitates memorization, confirms that the four lines constitute the oldest datable Christian creed:

> *Christ died for our sins in accordance with the scriptures,*
> *and he was buried;*
> *He has been raised on the third day in accordance with the scriptures,*
> *and he appeared to Peter and the Twelve.*

All new converts professed these basic beliefs. They were the touchstone of being a Christian, and guaranteed the unity of the Jesus movement.

Death

THE CREED HIGHLIGHTS not only the meaning of the death of Jesus, but the fact that he died. From a very early date enemies of Christianity found excuses to deny the resurrection. Either the body of Jesus had been stolen, or he had not really died at all. The first suggestion is absurd; why would his disciples play such a dangerous game, and then base their whole existence on a lie? The second has to be excluded, because Jesus died suspiciously early (Mark 15:44). The creed offers burial as the fundamental proof of death.

Only one scripture text relates human suffering culminating in death to benefit for others: "Ours were the sufferings he bore, ours the sorrows he carried . . . the punishment reconciling us fell on him, and we have been healed by his bruises" (Isaiah 53:4–6). Humanity merited punishment because of its corruption. In dying "for us" Christ assumed that terrible burden, and thereby introduced the human race into a new relationship with God. His death did not affect him alone; it was a salvific event that touched every human being. How precisely this works is spelled out by Paul in his pastoral advice in other contexts!

Resurrection

AS IN THE case of the death of Jesus, proof of his resurrection is offered; he appeared to Peter and others. We shall deal with this in the next section. Here the reference "according to the scriptures" is much more problematic. There is no reference in the Old Testament to the resurrection of the Messiah, nor is there any association of individual resurrection with "the third day." It seems likely, therefore, that a number of factors have been at work.

The phrase "on the third day" occurs so frequently in the Old Testament that it attracted the attention of the rabbis. From the fact that a whole series of individuals were "saved" on the third day, they deduced the principle, "The Holy One never leaves the righteous in distress more than three days" (Genesis Rabba on Genesis 42:17–18). The discovery of the empty tomb on the Sunday following Good Friday fitted so perfectly into this scriptural perspective that believers instinctively thought of the resurrection as occurring on the day of salvation.

This day in the past continues to influence the present. The Greek tense used, "he has been raised," evokes a completed action whose results continue to the time of writing. What is important is the state in which Christ found himself as the result of his resurrection. "He was constituted Son-of-God-in-power" (Romans 1:4). He became the Lord who saves today.

PRAYER

Lord, grant that when I say the creed I may believe in my heart what my lips pronounce.

THE WITNESSES

IN DISCUSSIONS OF the objective reality of the resurrection of Jesus, much is made of the fact that Paul does not mention the empty tomb. He appeals only to those who encountered the risen Jesus. Hence, the skeptics conclude, this is all there was. The disciples imagined everything. Nothing really happened.

Paul, of course, was much less naive than his modern critics. His concern was to reinforce the faith of his converts at Corinth about the middle of the year A.D. 54. Jesus, however, had died on April 7, A.D. 30. Even if there had been a body in the tomb on the following Sunday morning, it would have disintegrated into dust in the intervening twenty-four years! Elementary common sense indicated that an appeal to the empty tomb would have been pointless. Paul could only refer his readers to witnesses who were still alive.

The Experience of the Risen Lord

THE GREEK VERB used by Paul is often translated "he (the Risen Lord) was seen by Peter, etc." Contemporary usage, however, recommends that it be translated "he appeared to Peter, etc." The distinction is significant. The passive "was seen" emphasizes the subjective experience of the spectators. The active "he appeared," on the contrary, highlights the initiative of Jesus, and this is precisely what we find in the gospels. Jesus approaches Mary Magdalene (John 20:16). He erupts into the assembled disciples (John 20:19). He attaches himself to Cleopas and his companion (Luke 24:15).

The first disciples did not project their hopes. They had none! Mary weeps in grief (John 20:11). The disciples hide in fear (John 20:19). Cleopas confesses deep disappointment (Luke 24:21). Whatever Jesus might have said, his death was the end of their dreams. At this low moment, when they least expected it, someone took hold of them and changed their lives. The way the earliest appearance stories were told betrays the conviction of the earliest disciples that something real had happened to them. They were not hallucinating.

Available to Be Questioned

IN ALL PROBABILITY the appearance to Peter and the Twelve is that narrated in John 20:19–20. Others presumably were present, but the creed naturally singles out "official" figures.

Lest it might appear that he had an interest in citing only those who might be expected to uphold the party line, Paul adds a reference to the experience of 500 unnamed believers, some of whom are still alive and, by implication, available for questioning. The size of the crowd greatly reduces the plausibility of any suggestion that they deceived themselves. These were simple people whose lives were turned upside down by the experience. They had no position to uphold. But they could testify as to what had happened to them. The silence of the Gospels does not call this event into question.

No appearance to James, one of the four brothers of Jesus (Mark 6:3), is recorded in the Gospels. Something, however, must have happened to transform one who had refused to believe in Jesus (John 7:2–9) into a disciple (Acts 1:14) who progressively took over the leadership of the Jerusalem Church.

Personal reasons inspired Paul to single out James. The two had met on both of Paul's visits to Jerusalem, in A.D. 37 Galatians 1:19) and again in A.D. 51 (Galatians 2:9). James had concurred with Paul's conviction that Gentile converts to Christianity should not be circumcised. But it was the insistence of James that Jewish converts in Antioch must accept the most rigorous standard of dietary observance that forced Paul out of the church that had been his home (Galatians 2:11–14). Paul takes the opportunity to underline that James was not his superior. Their situations were identical! Both were converted after the resurrection and after a period of hostility to Jesus. Nonetheless both found a place among "all the apostles" who spread the gospel.

PRAYER
God, grant that in word and deed I may witness to the risen Lord.

PAUL'S CONVERSION

THE ONLY CLUE that Paul gives us as to the nature of his conversion is that he lists himself as the last witness to the risen Christ. His experience, therefore, was similar to that of others whose postresurrection recognition of Jesus is recorded in the Gospels. The four consistent elements in such stories provide us with a grid against which to analyze what happened to Paul on the road to Damascus.

Jesus' encounter with his disciples in John 20:19–20 is a typical recognition story, and the four elements are: (1) The disciples do not expect anything to happen; (2) Jesus takes the initiative by coming into their midst; (3) he gives them a sign of his identity by showing them his hands and his side; and (4) the disciples recognize the Lord. The two disciples on the way to Emmaus is another example of a recognition story (Luke 24:13–33).

Nothing Will Happen

PAUL'S LETTERS PRESENT his persecution of Christians as evidence of his zeal for the Jewish Law (Philippians 3:6; Galatians 1:13–14). In consequence, it was not a duty imposed on him but a personal choice which, moreover, set him apart from other Pharisees (Philippians 3:5). According to the Acts of the Apostles, only Sadducees displayed hostility to Christianity in Jerusalem.

Paul's motives, however, were as mysterious as his reason for going to Damascus. As he neared the city he never anticipated that anything would happen. The Jesus movement was a divisive factor at a time when Jewish unity was becoming ever more important in the face of the threat of Rome. But he had dismissed Jesus as a false teacher who had led Jews astray, perhaps by faking miracles (2 Corinthians 5:16). Paul certainly never dreamed of an encounter with a man who had died the horrible death of crucifixion. The idea that God would raise from the dead a false Messiah who had subverted the Jewish Law was blasphemous.

The Encounter

IT WAS JESUS who moved to find Paul. The emotion of the moment still resonates in "I was laid hold of by Christ Jesus" (Philippians 3:12). Paul was swept off his feet. How did he know that it was Jesus of Nazareth? Other disciples had known Jesus during his earthly lifetime and could make the connection with the postresurrection figure. Even though Paul had been in Jerusalem during the years when Jesus taught and died there, no hint exists that they ever met. The basis of recognition, therefore, is a problem. If, however, simple interest in a book can generate a mental picture of the author, Paul's anger may have developed an image of Jesus, particularly since hatred interfered with his thought processes and heightened his susceptibility.

The Energy of a New Convert

NOTHING IN PAUL'S life called for the divine intervention that made him a follower of Christ. Such pure unmerited love thereafter colored his understanding of God's relationship with humanity; for example, "God shows his love for us in that while we were yet sinners Christ died for us" (Romans 5:8).

Paul's response to such free grace was to cooperate fully with it. In his dictionary, "to work, to labor" meant to minister in the service of the gospel, a factor that must be kept in mind in order to appreciate properly the role of the women listed in Romans 16:1–16. Those with whom Paul compares himself are not only men.

What Paul did in his enthusiasm was to rush off to preach in Arabia (Galatians 1:17), today the northern part of Jordan. Perhaps that experience taught him how ill-prepared he was, and for the next three years he preached in Damascus (Galatians 1:18) while he learned the trade that would give him the financial independence that made it possible for him to travel widely. Everywhere he went, he and all the other apostles preached that Christ died for us and rose on the third day.

PRAYER

God, make me aware of all the graces you give me, and enable me to return your love by laboring in your service.

IF THERE IS NO RESURRECTION

PAUL RECEIVED FIRST-CLASS training in public speaking. This involved instruction in how to organize material in order to argue a case effectively. Logic obviously played a key role in such presentations. Thus far in this letter, few of Paul's responses to the problems at Corinth have been remarkable for their rational structure. Here, however, we see how devastating his logic could be.

Identifying with Opponents

WHEN DEALING WITH 15:1–2 we saw that all Greeks and most cultivated Jews did not believe in resurrection of the body. For them the body was a drag on the soul, and at death the soul escaped into immortality. Not surprisingly, therefore, some Corinthians took the position, "There is no such thing as resurrection."

Paul begins by pointing out the absurdity of this thesis. In professing the creed (15:3–5), the Corinthians accepted that Jesus Christ had been raised from the dead. If one person had passed through death to life with a body, then the possibility of resurrection cannot be denied. Today it would be extremely foolish to deny that humans can walk on the moon, because several have actually done it. What is real must be possible.

Having scored a decisive point, Paul with apparent magnanimity (he is in fact going to slaughter his opponents) says, "Let us assume for the sake of the argument that you are correct and that the dead are not raised. What consequences necessarily follow?"

The Consequences of Denying Resurrection

IF RESURRECTION IS not a possibility, as the Corinthians maintained, then survival after death cannot involve a body. There can be no exceptions to what is absolutely impossible. For example, unaided flight is impossible for human beings, thus Superman hurtling through the sky cannot be real.

Similarly, in Corinthian terms, Christ cannot have been raised from the dead.

It is not necessary to assume that the Corinthians denied that Christ survived death, and is still alive. Their point would be that, whatever the appearances, those who thought of his survival in terms of resurrection were wrong. Paul, however, does not pursue this interesting sideline. He keeps to a strict logical line, where each step is a consequence of the one before.

If Christ cannot have been raised from the dead, then Paul has been preaching falsehood. He has laid himself open to the accusation of misrepresenting God, whose emissary he is (1:1), because he solemnly proclaimed that God raised Christ. While this argument might have brought tears to the eyes of Paul's most fervent supporters, it would have cut very little ice with the rest of the community. The partisans of Apollos considered Paul incompetent as a spiritual leader, and Paul's verbal brutality toward the intellectuals at Corinth in the first chapters of this letter would have alienated some of those whose instinct would have been to side with him.

The weakness of this argument, however, was designed to lull the Corinthians into a false sense of security while Paul prepared the killing stroke: "You believed me!"

Everything the Corinthians enjoyed—friendship with God, redemption in Christ, the gifts of the Spirit—rested on their acceptance of Paul's gospel, of which the resurrection of Christ was the linchpin. The new life they lived was caused by that gospel. But if that gospel was false, then it had no power to change anything. The distinction between "being saved" and "perishing" was meaningless (1:18). The Corinthians were just ordinary sinners, exactly like everyone else. This, of course, is the last thing the elite at Corinth would want to hear.

Finally, the dead family and friends with whom they had hoped to be united in the next life were lost forever. This, of course, did not follow for those who believed in immortality. But they had only theory. Paul had a fact. It is the resurrection of Christ that made the possible real. If we only "hope" that Christ survived death we are like children whistling in the dark to keep up their courage.

PRAYER
God, may I truly believe that Christ rose from the dead.
Help my unbelief!

IF ONE THEN ALL

AFTER THE STICK, the carrot! Paul has used his incisive logic to reduce the Corinthians to despair by outlining with ruthless clarity the consequences of their denial of the possibility of resurrection (15:12–19). The same logic, fortunately, can be used for more beneficial purposes. Paul now begins to show that if the resurrection of Christ is accepted, there will be life beyond death for others.

From Possibility to Fact

THE DOCTRINAIRE APPROACH of the Corinthians with respect to the irrelevance of the body had blinded them to the significance of the resurrection of Christ. They interpreted his survival after death in terms of their theory of immortality. For Paul this was putting the cart before the horse.

An eminent English historian once wrote, "What man can do is what man has done." A rather silly remark at first sight, but it is in fact very profound. It specifies the only way we know something to be really possible. Theories and calculations, however plausible, are meaningless beside the question: Has someone actually done it? We know that the 1500 meters can be run in the time of the current world record. Can it be done in three minutes? We won't know until someone does it.

This highly pragmatic perspective is the one in which Paul views the resurrection of Christ. Prior to that event, individual survival after death was a deduction based on the goodness of God (see 15:1–2). The solidity of the premise and the quality of the logic seemed to be beyond question. But there was always a nagging doubt since "God's ways are not our ways." True in Judaism, this was accentuated in Christianity, a religion based on a crucified savior: "Has not God made foolish the wisdom of the world?" (1:20). The importance of the resurrection of Christ for Paul was that it removed any doubt regarding the feasibility of life after death. The raising of Christ transformed resurrection from a possibility into a fact. One man had done it!

All believers now know with confidence that they *can be raised* from the dead. Paul, however, goes a step further. Those who have died (15:18) *will be raised* from the dead. Christ is only the first among many. How did Paul know that the resurrection of Christ was not a unique case?

Adam and Christ

FOR PAUL, CHRIST was above all the New Adam. He was what Adam was intended to be. In his self-sacrificing love Christ exhibited the humanity that God desired, whereas the self-centeredness of Adam defeated the divine purpose. Thus if Adam's life had implications for all humanity, so must the life of Christ. The purpose of his mission was the salvation of all.

From the book of Genesis Paul knew that Adam's sin had unleashed a force of evil that increasingly affected all humanity (Genesis 1–11). Each generation, by accepting false values, passed them on reinforced to the next. The distortion that Adam introduced into the pattern of human existence is highlighted by the universal fact of death. "God did not make death, and he does not delight in the death of the living" (Wisdom 1:12).

As the New Adam, Christ had the mission to undo the damage caused by Adam. If Adam was responsible for death, then Christ must give life. The causality of Adam, however, is automatic. We belong to Adam by birth. We have no choice but to be born into a society distorted by false values. Whether we like it or not we are carried along like chips of wood on a fast-flowing stream. Death we cannot avoid.

The life Christ gives, on the other hand, is not automatic. It benefits only those who believe in him and have committed themselves to him. We belong to Christ only by choice. Salvation is the gift of life both here and through eternity.

PRAYER
Lord, never let me doubt the reality of life after death.

How History Will Unroll

THE TONE CHANGES so radically that Paul's readers must have felt that they were on an emotional roller-coaster. Cool, incisive logic gives way to the passion of a prophet who soars into the future, fervently declaring a conviction that transcends reason and experience. The hope Paul has inspired merges into a magnificent vision of faith.

For those, like Paul, with a traditional Jewish background, the resurrection of the dead was one of the signs that present history had entered its final phase (Matthew 27:51–53). From this perspective, the raising of Jesus set in motion an inexorable succession of events culminating in the return of Jesus to the Father to report his mission completed.

The Stages

THE RAISING OF Jesus is the beginning of the last phase of human history. It is the decisive break with a past in which death was all-powerful, and the herald of a new future in which life is eternal.

This future, however, does not yet exist insofar as all Christians are concerned. They do not pass directly from this life to the next. Christ's resurrection is a pledge of what is to come. It is a guarantee that they will rise from the dead. But meanwhile they have to live and die in hope.

The period of waiting will end when Christ returns in glory. Paul gave a graphic description of this moment in his first letter: "The Lord himself will descend from heaven with a cry of command . . . and the dead in Christ will arise first. Then we who are alive, who are left, shall be caught up together with them in the clouds to meet the Lord in the air. And so we shall always be with the Lord" (1 Thessalonians 4:16–17).

Triumph Over Death

THE PHRASE "THEN comes the End" (15:24) has given rise to a lot of discussion. Some have argued that it means "finally the remainder [of the dead]." This translation would imply an earthly messianic kingdom, in which Christ and his risen followers enjoy terrestrial bliss for an unspecified period, culminating in a second resurrection of all the non-Christian dead. This prospect is very inviting to a certain type of mind for which speculation on the conditions of life in such a kingdom takes precedence over loving one's neighbor.

A thousand-year kingdom, however, has no basis in the text. The best translation of the key phrase is "thereupon the goal (of Christ's mission) is achieved." The general resurrection of believers *is* the triumph of life over death (15:54). The escape of so many from its clutches shows that death no longer reigns over human life. What appeared to be death's omnipotence is revealed by the power of Christ to be a sham.

Death is personified as the ultimate force hostile to human happiness. Its tentacles, however, reach out into daily life. In keeping with the spirit of his time, Paul speaks of evil powers. Their names are unimportant, and cannot be attached to specific beings. Paul sees them as facets of death because they are essentially destructive. They create nothing, but anticipate and prepare for the final dissolution. The void left by lack of love is the emptiness of death.

The Surrender of the Kingdom

THE IMPORTANCE THAT Paul gives to Christ should not blind us to the fact that he is entirely dependent on God. Christ did not rise from the dead by his own power. He was raised by God. Christ is the Son who was sent by the Father (Galatians 4:4). God is the source of his saving power, and of his title "Lord" (Philippians 2:9–11). In the last analysis, therefore, Christ must return his mandate, and all that he achieved by it, to God.

PRAYER
God, help me to eradicate the traces of death in my conduct so that I may cooperate in Christ's conquest of death.

STRUGGLE A SIGN

WITHOUT ANY WARNING Paul changes his tactics once again. He has tried logical argument and impassioned appeal. Having soared to the heavens, he now swoops down to the mundane. Would he live the sort of life he leads if he were not absolutely convinced of the fact of the resurrection of Christ? The message to the intellectuals at Corinth is clear. If they were incapable of appreciating the force of his arguments, they could at least reflect on the implications of his commitment.

Baptism for the Dead

IF THE STANDARD English translation of 15:29 is taken at face value, it means that members of the Church at Corinth were having themselves baptized a second, third, or fourth time for friends or members of their families who had died before becoming Christians.

Paul, we are told by those who accept this translation, argues that the sole possible justification for such a practice is his teaching that only those who have been baptized, and so belong to Christ (15:23), will be raised from the dead. Those who were not Christians will not be raised to eternal life (what happens to them is not Paul's concern at this point). In other words, Paul triumphantly points out a contradiction. Resurrection is both affirmed and denied by the Corinthians! Their deeds and their words do not harmonize.

The difficulty with this interpretation is that Paul's understanding of the way sacraments work would never have permitted him to condone such superstition in any of his churches. Submission to the rite of baptism benefits the individual because it externalizes a personal decision for Christ. The dead cannot make the act of faith that saves (Romans 10:9).

Working Themselves to Death

A RADICALLY DIFFERENT interpretation becomes possible if the key words are recognized as having multiple meanings (for example, "to baptize" in Greek commonly meant "to destroy, to perish"), and if we remember that Paul in this letter regularly quotes from the letter of the Corinthians (7:1).

In this hypothesis the Corinthians said of Paul and his collaborators, "Why are they destroying themselves on account of 'the dead'?" In reply Paul reinforced the thrust of the argument in order to make his response even more devastating; "If those who are really dead are not raised, why are people being destroyed on their account?"

The intellectuals at Corinth, among whom were those who denied the resurrection, mocked Paul and his team for the effort they expended on those whom they considered "dead" to higher spiritual things. Paul was being ground down by a concern that they deemed pointless. He was being destroyed by a commitment that they considered futile.

The intellectuals' use of "dead" to mean those whom they despised in the community played straight into Paul's hands. In his reply, as in 2:6–16, he changes the meaning of their words. He takes "dead" literally and relates it to resurrection. The Corinthians had conceded that he and his collaborators were killing themselves. But what they preached highlighted the resurrection (15:1–5). "Therefore," Paul implies, "you should conclude that we must be totally convinced that Christ is risen. Otherwise why should we waste our lives?"

Just in case the Corinthians failed to get the point, Paul introduces a graphic image, "fighting with beasts at Ephesus." This cannot be taken literally, if only because Paul survived to tell about it! It was a common metaphor for a highly dangerous situation (2 Timothy 4:17), just as being "thrown to the lions" is in today's reporting on debates in the House of Representatives. The unknown danger at Ephesus (16:8) was simply another example of the stressful situations that made up Paul's life. He struggles on only because he is convinced that the resurrection of Christ makes a difference for everyone. If there was no resurrection, it would be more sensible to turn to drink.

PRAYER
Lord, let my life betray my conviction that the dead will rise.

THE RESURRECTION BODY

WITH IMMENSE SKILL Paul varies the tone and texture of his presentation in order to ensure that his audience will not get bored during this long argument in favor of the resurrection. A torrent of rhetorical questions (15:29–34) here gives way to a real question that would have been in everyone's mind.

Paul dramatizes the situation by using direct speech. We should imagine someone in the audience trying to score off Paul by asking an unanswerable question. "Very well, let us assume that the dead are raised. Then they must have bodies. They cannot possibly be our present bodies because the dead exist in a completely different world. So what are resurrection bodies like?" Hostility can be deduced from Paul's exasperated retort, "You foolish person!"

Paul, of course, in the moment of his conversion had encountered someone with a resurrection body (15:8), but was too shrewd to answer in such terms knowing that his audience, who had not fully accepted his arguments, would be thinking of friends and relatives who had moldered in their graves for several years.

Words Do Not Always Have the Same Meaning

PAUL BEGINS WITH a series of illustrations designed to force the Corinthians to recall what everyone knew, but whose relevance to the issue of resurrection had escaped them.

An acorn has to be planted in the ground, where it changes radically before becoming a mighty oak tree. The acorn has a body and the tree has a body. They are in no way similar, yet they are the same thing. The tree-body is determined by God, but no one could anticipate his intention from the seed-body, particularly since the seeds of different species look alike. Hence, Paul implies, it is perfectly feasible for us to conceive ourselves as existing in an entirely different body, even if we cannot imagine what it will look like.

The main thing, Paul continues, is to stop thinking that words like "body" and "flesh" always mean the same thing. The "flesh" of humans differs from that of animals, which differs from that of birds, which differs from that of fish. These are all earthly "bodies" but we also talk of heavenly "bodies," the sun, moon, and stars, whose composition is entirely different. The heavenly bodies all shine but the "radiance" ("glory") of the sun is completely different from that of the moon. Even the stars differ among themselves in the "radiance" they emit. In sum, the realities to which we apply terms like "body" may not be the only ones to which such terms can be applied.

Imagining a Resurrection Body

HAVING THUS OPENED the minds of his audience to an unexpected use of "body," Paul invites them to speculate on the minimum qualities a resurrection body should have. Obviously nothing that makes the present body a burden can be retained. It must be replaced by a positive quality.

Very quickly Paul draws up a list on which everyone would agree. He very cleverly links opposites by "sow" to remind the audience of the radical change in the seed when planted.

Present Body	Resurrection Body
Perishable	Imperishable
Dishonor	Glory
Weakness	Power
Material/Physical	Spiritual

The only pair that is not immediately intelligible is "dishonor–glory." "Glory" here is the righteousness-in-splendor that Adam and Eve enjoyed before the Fall. Being all that God desired them to be, they gave "glory" to their Creator. Their descendants, however, "sinned and fall short of the glory of God" (Romans 3:23). "Inglorious" would be better than "dishonor." Believers here and now are being transformed "from glory to glory" (2 Corinthians 3:18) as their behavior becomes ever more Christlike, and the process will continue in the next life. The risen body of Christ is "glorious" (Philippians 3:21).

PRAYER

Lord, grant me the flexibility of mind to persevere with difficult
theological ideas.

THERE WILL BE A
RESURRECTION BODY

AS PAUL ELABORATED his argument in the previous section, there were those among his audience who were delighted at the line he was taking. It appeared to lead straight to a decisive objection. If, as Paul had insisted, what is factual must be possible (see 15:20), there is no guarantee that what is possible is real. All that Paul did was to create an ideal mirror image of the present defective body. What proof is there, his opponents asked, that it actually exists? Their question is perfectly reasonable. Do we today take the flights of fancy of science fiction authors as description of reality?

Two Creation Narratives

ONCE AGAIN PAUL has lured his opponents into a false sense of security. He has anticipated the objection, and replies bluntly, "If there is a physical body, there is also a spiritual body" (15:44).

His argument appears strange to us but would have been understandable to his contemporaries, particularly those of the Apollos party at Corinth. These had been influenced by the thinking of Philo, the greatest representative of Jewish-Greek philosophy. Genesis has two creation accounts. In the first, God creates man in his own image (1:27), whereas in the second he forms him from the dust of the earth and makes him a living being (2:7). Philo, therefore, distinguished two men: "The heavenly man, as being born in the image of God, has no participation in any corruptible or earthlike essence. But the earthly man is made of loose material, which he calls a lump of clay" (*Allegorical Interpretation* 1:31).

This distinction offered Paul two advantages. It provided the basis of the two terms he needed ("spiritual" and "physical"). The heavenly man was obviously entirely "spiritual," and the earthly man was completely "physical." Secondly it located both figures at the beginning of time.

First and Last Adam

IN A LITERARY arrangement called an "inclusion," often found in the Bible, the end of a story corresponds to the beginning. Luke's version of Jesus' agony at Gethsemane, for example, begins and ends with the words "Pray that you may not enter into temptation" (22:40, 46). On a much grander scale, Jews believed that the end of history would correspond to its beginning. What God gave would return to him (15:28).

Believing that the resurrection of Christ had inaugurated the last period of history, this principle enabled Paul to transpose Philo's distinction from the beginning of time to the present, while reversing the order. The last is the mirror image of the first. If in creation the order was "spiritual," then "physical," so in the last age the order would be "physical," then "spiritual." Hence, the present existence of a "physical" body necessarily implies that there will be a "spiritual" body. Undergirding this rather tortuous logic, it goes without saying, is Paul's absolute conviction that Christ actually exists in a spiritual dimension.

In developing this theme Paul shifts his ground slightly, and contrasts the different ways of existing in a "physical" or "spiritual" body in terms of the First Adam and the Last Adam, who of course is Christ, although this is never stated. The former was a life-receiving "soul" (*psyche*, a word related to the term translated "physical" in this and the previous section). The latter is a life-giving spirit, as a result of his resurrection; "he was constituted Son-of-God-in-power according to the spirit of holiness by his resurrection from the dead" (Romans 1:4).

Paul's reason for singling out Adam and Christ is that they are representative figures. Each has a determining influence on others. The relationship of humanity to Adam and that of believers to Christ has already been spelled out in 15:22. The first is a matter of necessity; as he is dust, so are we. The second is a matter of choice. Hence, Paul concludes with an exhortation, "Let us also bear the likeness of the man from heaven." To belong to Christ is the only guarantee of a "spiritual" body.

PRAYER

Lord, having received the life of the Spirit, may I communicate it to others.

THOSE WHO ARE STILL ALIVE

IN DISCUSSING MARRIAGE Paul had revealed his conviction that "the appointed time has grown very short" (7:29). He believed that it would not be long until Christ returned in glory and the dead were raised (15:23). He fully expected to be around to see it. He had briefly considered this climactic moment in his first letter, but there he said only, "Then we who are still alive, who are left, shall be caught up with them [those who have already died] in the clouds to meet the Lord in the air" (1 Thessalonians 4:17). The image that immediately comes to mind is that of a cloud of leaves being swept up in a whirlwind. It does not seem that Paul had given much thought to precisely how it was going to work.

The Need for Transformation

THE THOROUGH REFLECTION forced upon Paul by the Corinthians' denial of the resurrection obliged him to confront the problem of survivors explicitly. It had been relatively easy for him to deal with the question of believers who had already died. Their situation was clarified by the "sown seed" metaphor. They would be buried with one sort of body, and rise with another. But what about believers who would not be "sown" in the grave, who would be alive when Christ appeared?

At this stage Paul was clear that if "flesh and blood" was appropriate for existence in this present world, it must be inappropriate for the world to come. Even though some believers do not die, their fate cannot be different from that of dead believers, because they all bear the image of the man of heaven. Thus they must somehow acquire a "spiritual" body.

Understandably, Paul does not tell us how this is going to come about. He is sure, however, that it will happen very quickly, "in the blink of an eye," and he distracts his audience by evoking the last great trumpet blast which was a standard feature of the Day of Yahweh in Jewish literature (Joel 2:1; Zephaniah 1:16).

Paul's rhetorical training betrays itself again in the rhythmic repetition of antithetical terms: "What is corruptible must put on incorruptibility, and the mortal must put on immortality."

Victory Over Death

ONCE ALL BELIEVERS are clothed in incorruptibility and immortality, death can no longer touch them. Paul celebrates this victory by using two passages of the Old Testament which personify death, Isaiah 25:8 and Hosea 13:14, to clothe his own thoughts. The second text is originally a threat. Death is invited to slay unfaithful Jews. Paul, however, uses the same words as a taunt. Placing himself at the end of time he mocks a now powerless death, as people relieved from fear revile a fallen dictator.

Although 15:56 is typically Pauline, I doubt very much that Paul wrote it here. Not only is it anticlimactic, but nothing in this letter has prepared us for the highly charged language, and the ideas are explained only in the epistle to the Romans. "Death," "sin," and "Law" are the key elements in Paul's vision of a world without Christ. "Sin" is the world in the false orientation given humanity by the sin of Adam. One of the most important manifestations of the power of "sin" was an exaggerated respect for the "Law," which expressed itself in blind obedience. This loss of the responsibility of freedom transformed humans to nonpersons, whose way of being is "death."

One can see why an editor would want to temper Paul's euphoria by reminding believers for whom the return of Christ has been long delayed that they have to live in a world whose false values must be resisted if they are to come to resurrection.

Paul's conclusion, however, does not emphasize good behavior but ministry. Believers must spread the good news of the resurrection. They have not believed in vain (15:2) and they will not labor in vain (15:58), a neat ending to a long and complex argument.

PRAYER
Lord, save me from sin, death, and the Law.

COLLECTION FOR JERUSALEM

HAVING DEALT WITH all the substantive issues in the community at Corinth that had come to his attention through the unofficial report of Chloe's people and the official delegation, Paul wraps up his letter with a number of housekeeping items.

The Need for the Collection

ALL THE GREAT cities of antiquity had very high unemployment, and Jerusalem was no exception. In fact it was probably worse, because idleness was encouraged by the fact that alms-giving was considered particularly meritorious when done in the Holy City.

From the beginning the Christian community in Jerusalem had to worry about poverty among its members. "Those who possessed land or houses sold them, and brought the proceeds of what was sold and laid it at the apostles' feet, and distribution was made to each as had any need" (Acts 4:34–35). Obviously this system of internal relief could be maintained only as long as there was a continuing influx of new rich converts into the community. As the Church began to distance itself from Judaism, institutional sources of external relief began to dry up.

A crisis was fast approaching when Paul and Barnabas came to Jerusalem in the autumn of A.D. 51 in order to deal with the question of whether pagan converts to Christianity should be circumcised or not. The decision not to circumcise them went in Paul's favor, and he heartily assented to the appeal of the leaders of the Jerusalem Church to send money (Galatians 2:10).

Paul's Attitude

WHEN HE ACCEPTED this responsibility Paul was not speaking for himself but for the Church of Antioch, whose representative he was. Sometime during the following winter, Jewish believers at Antioch effectively obliged Gentile members to become Jews if the unity of the Church was to be maintained. Paul could not accept this, and left Antioch the following spring, never to return. He definitively broke his links with the Church there.

Nonetheless he assumed the burden of the collection for Jerusalem as a personal commitment. His motives were perhaps complex. Having lived in Jerusalem as a Pharisee for nearly twenty years, he knew the social situation at first hand. Moreover, the discussion about circumcision in Jerusalem and what happened subsequently at Antioch forced him to realize that his churches, comprised in the great majority of converts from paganism, were drifting away from the essentially Jewish Church in Jerusalem. Aid from the more prosperous Gentile churches was one way of bridging the gap, and he did not want his churches to lose sight of their roots in Palestine.

Practical Instructions

PAUL BEGGED THE Galatians to participate in the collection when he spent the summer of A.D. 52 with them in the course of his long walk from Antioch to Ephesus, which was to be his base for the next two years or so.

Paul does not appear to have preached about the collection in Corinth. The impression given here is that the community there somehow heard of the project, perhaps from Apollos or Chloe's people, and wanted to participate, but did not know what time scale Paul had in mind or how he wanted things organized. So they asked him in their letter (7:1).

Utterly opposed to binding moral precepts (Philemon 14), Paul had no compunction about laying down the law in administrative matters. The Corinthians were to set something aside every week—the implication is that everyone had some surplus wealth—because the size of the collection was important. An insignificant sum would have been an insult that widened the breach between Jerusalem and the Pauline churches. In a world where everyone who could possibly do so dipped their fingers in the till, Paul protected his reputation by insisting that Corinth should select from its members those who would carry the money to Jerusalem. He would go with them, or accredit them as the case might be, in order that Jerusalem should know that he had fulfilled his promise. A year was to go by before the Corinthians did anything (2 Corinthians 8–9).

PRAYER
Lord, give me the grace actually to do something to help the poor.

TRAVEL PLANS

IN DEALING WITH the organization of the collection for the poor of Jerusalem, Paul did not say when he planned to arrive in Corinth (16:1–4). Realizing a little tardily that it was important for the Corinthians to know how much time they had to get together a sum that would do honor to a city known throughout the ancient world as "wealthy Corinth," he now goes into his travel plans in more detail.

Events in Ephesus

PAUL HAD NOW been in Ephesus, the capital of the Roman province of Asia, for almost two years (Acts 19:8–10). The Christian community, which had been founded by his aides Prisca and Aquila (Acts 18:19), had grown steadily. His policy of converting those who came to the capital on business and sending them back to their hometowns as missionaries had proved very successful. Epaphras, for example, had founded the Church at Colossae (Colossians 1:7).

There had also been serious problems internally and externally. The community at Ephesus was split into supporters and opponents of Paul. The latter presumably resented his taking over the direction of a Church that had in fact been established by others. While he was being held in the governor's residence pending investigation, they used the opportunity to show him that he was not really needed (Philippians 1:12–26).

Hurtful as this contempt was to Paul personally, he was much more concerned about the activities of his erstwhile colleagues at Antioch. The Church there had decided that the communities founded by Paul when he was a missionary of Antioch should be transformed into the same Jewish mold as the mother Church. Paul already had to deal with the havoc such troublemakers (from his point of view) had created in Galatia, and he feared greatly that Philippi, Thessalonica, and Corinth would be next on the list.

A Swing Through Macedonia

THIS DANGEROUS DEVELOPMENT explains why Paul needed to visit his Macedonian churches in Philippi and Thessalonica before going to Corinth. He appears to have written this letter sometime after Easter (5:7), which in A.D. 54 fell on April 12, but did not plan to move from Ephesus until after Pentecost, which fell on June 2.

His anticipated route was straightforward. A Roman road ran north to Troas where ships plied to Neapolis (modern Kevalla), the port of Philippi. At that point he was on the Via Egnatia, the great Roman road running across northern Greece and southern Albania to the Adriatic coast. Thessalonica was three days walk west of Philippi on this road. The road south to Athens was not as good but was well traveled. Paul estimated that he would be in Corinth before the onset of winter. It would have been a very busy summer, and he would have walked almost 700 miles.

This plan, however, came to nothing. Circumstances forced Paul to rush to Corinth shortly after this letter was written.

Timothy and Apollos

TIMOTHY HAD ALREADY left for Corinth (4:17) to check on the rumors brought by Chloe's people concerning certain bizarre practices in the community. Earlier in this letter Paul had betrayed his worry as to how Timothy would be received, and the same concern surfaces here. Even though Timothy knew the Corinthians well, having spent a year and a half there during the foundation of the Church (Acts 18:5, 11), Paul was fully aware that the contempt some members of the community had for him might rub off on his envoy, who was specifically sent to remind them of Paul's way of doing things.

Why Apollos left Corinth we do no know. It is not impossible that he did not like the way his teaching was being interpreted to put him into opposition with Paul. In order not to fuel the divisions in the community (1:12), Paul goes out of his way to suggest that there were no disagreements between them (3:6), and that he was not responsible for the failure of Apollos to return to Corinth.

PRAYER
Lord, help me to take the responsibilities of friendship seriously, and to stay in touch and to give aid when needed.

EMERGING LEADERS

As PAUL CAME to the end of each of his letters, he realized that it would be some time before he would be in communication again with that church. Had he said everything that needed to be said? Hence he normally concludes with a flurry of last-minute instructions, exactly like a worried mother sending a young child off to school on a snowy day.

The five imperatives (16:13–14) deal with the two most basic elements of the Christian life: faith and love. The first four carry essentially the same message: remain faithful to the gospel as you received if from me. In his heart of hearts, Paul (perhaps mistakenly) believed that the Corinthians had grasped what he wanted them to hear. All they had to do was act with the courge of their convictions, and not be swayed by those with different ideas. The fifth imperative reminds them that love must be the guiding force in all they did.

Values and Structures

LOVING ONE'S NEIGHBOR and shared prayer are two obvious examples of the sort of values that should be accepted by every Christian community. These values can be expressed in a number of different structures. Loving one's neighbor can take the form of finding work for someone unemployed or of providing a hot meal for a sick person. The value of shared prayer comes to life in the choral recitation of the psalms in a monastic community as well as in the charismatic prayer of a lay group.

Paul believed that each local church should determine its own structures. It was his job to teach his converts what values were important and to inspire them to make these part of their lives. It was also his responsibility to challenge them if he felt that they were not taking certain fundamental values seriously. Equally, however, Paul was convinced that it would be wrong for him to spell out structures that a community should observe. He felt so strongly about this point because he had seen what the Law had done to the lives of Jews.

If parents make every decision for their growing children, those children will never become mature adults. Because of the way that the Jews had permitted the Law's directives to dictate every facet of their lives, it condemned them to prison and cost them their freedom (Galatians 3:23–24). Paul was not prepared to permit the same thing to happen to his churches. He had to safeguard their freedom, which meant not telling them what to do.

Leadership

LEADERSHIP IS A necessary value. No community can survive without it. Paul, however, could not determine the type of leadership or name the individuals who would exercise it. That would be to undermine the independence of the community in the choice of its own structures. All that Paul could do was to commend to each community those of its members who had emerged and been accepted as leaders.

Thus in his very first letter Paul tells the Thessalonians "to respect those who labor among you and are over you in the Lord and admonish you, and to esteem them very highly in love because of their work" (1 Thessalonians 5:12–13). These individuals had taken the initiative in concern for the quality of life of the community. Their success showed that they were gifted by the Holy Spirit for this role (12:28). In the same vein he directs the Philippians 3:17).

Similarly here Paul simply points out to the Corinthians that Stephanas, Fortunatus, and Achaicus should be recognized as leaders by the community because of all that they had done for it. "They have devoted themselves to the service of the saints" (16:15). He had obviously been impressed by their performance as they worked on the problems of the Church they represented.

PRAYER
God, may the Church cease believing that ordination confers the gift of leadership, and that the dictation of structures promotes values.

FINAL GREETINGS

THE SLIGHTLY POMPOUS gesture of sending greetings from "the churches of Asia" was no doubt prompted by Paul's sense of occasion. After all, he was writing from Ephesus (16:8), the capital of the Roman province of Asia, to Corinth, the main commercial center of Greece. Unconsciously he betrays the success of his ministry at Ephesus. These churches were the result of the sort of missionary outreach that led to the foundation of the Church at Colossae.

Prisca and Aquila

THE SUDDEN SHIFT from solemn official greetings to the warm good wishes of a couple has a very simple explanation. Prisca and Aquila were with Paul as the letter was being finished, and noticed that there was space at the bottom of the page. They urged him to greet the Corinthians on their behalf, and he indulgently complied. The little exchange illustrates the close relationship of the couple and the apostle.

Originally from Pontus on the south coast of the Black Sea, Aquila married Prisca in Rome and set up a tentmaking business. On becoming Christians they found themselves embroiled in a synagogue dispute concerning Christ which became a public scandal. The emperor Claudius stepped in, closed the synagogue, and expelled its members from Rome. Prisca and Aquila moved to Corinth, where the Isthmian Games (see 9:24–27) guaranteed plenty of work. There they hired Paul to work with them (Acts 18:1–3).

This invitation changed Paul's missionary strategy. Prior to this, when he went into a new town he had nothing already arranged. He had to find work and lodgings, and then build up a network of contacts. At Corinth, Prisca and Aquila provided him with all these. He could begin a productive apostolate immediately. When Paul decided that Ephesus would be his next missionary base—it was the center of a circle containing all his foundations—he sent Prisca and Aquila there to begin operations (Acts

18:19) while he went back to Antioch and Jerusalem (Galatians 2:1–10). By the time he joined them a year later things were running smoothly.

After Timothy, the couple were his closest collaborators. Not only did they risk their lives but they also made big financial sacrifices for his sake. To close down a business and start again in a strange city cost money. Subsequently, he uprooted them from Ephesus to prepare for his arrival in Rome. As Paul himself acknowledged, all the Gentile churches owed them a debt of gratitude (Romans 16:3–4).

Authenticating a Letter

PAUL COULD CERTAINLY write, but whenever possible he employed a secretary. The only one we know by name is Tertius, who penned Romans (Romans 16:22). Not only could such a professional write much more quickly than Paul, but his script would certainly be neater and more legible. On one occasion Paul excuses his large awkward letters (Galatians 6:11). Moreover, a first-class secretary was trained in shorthand symbols and could take dictation at the speed of normal speech, leaving Paul free to move around and gesture as he composed a letter.

Since the secretary might not always be the same person, it could happen that a community got letters from Paul written in different hands. How could they know that they were genuine? Forgeries were not unknown (2 Thessalonians 2:2). The only way was to have Paul pen the last paragraph personally: "I, Paul, write this greeting with my own hand. This is the mark in every letter of mine. It is the way I write" (2 Thessalonians 3:17).

This is the only letter-ending to contain a curse. It is directed against all those who do not love Jesus, and the form is a last attempt to jolt the Corinthians into recognition of the fundamental importance of the Crucified One. They in effect had said "Jesus be cursed" (12:3) when they neglected the lesson of his life. Now Paul insists not that they must obey, but that they must love as Jesus did. A fitting conclusion to a letter that contains chapter 13.

PRAYER
God, let us be truly grateful for authors like Paul, and secretaries like Tertius.

FOLLOW-UP READING

Background

J. Murphy-O'Connor, *St. Paul's Corinth, Texts and Archaeology*. Good News Studies 6, 2nd edition, Liturgical Press, Collegeville, Minn., 1992. Collects and translates all the Greek and Latin references to Corinth and combines them with the results of a century of archaeological excavations to create a vivid picture of the first-century city.

J. Murphy-O'Connor, *Paul the Letter-Writer. His World, His Options, His Skills*. Good News Studies 41, Liturgical Press, Collegeville, Minn., 1995. Deals with writing materials, the qualifications of secretaries, and the way letters were organized in antiquity.

J. Murphy-O'Connor, *Paul. A Critical Life*. Clarendon Press, Oxford, 1996. Chapters 11 and 12 explore in detail Paul's relations with the Church at Corinth, and highlight the facets of his personality that his correspondence reveals.

Commentaries

C. K. Barrett, *The First Epistle to the Corinthians*. Black's New Testament Commentaries, Black, London, 1968. Written with extraordinary clarity and perception, this is still the best popular commentary.

G. D. Fee, *The First Epistle to the Corinthians*. The New International Commentary on the New Testament, Eerdmans, Grand Rapids, Mich., 1987. A scientific commentary characterized by a consistent effort to follow the precise articulation of Paul's thought, but with a developed evangelical pastoral dimension.

J. J. Kilgallen, *First Corinthians. An Introduction and Study Guide*. Paulist Press, New York/Mahwah, 1987. A painless introduction which communicates all the excitement of what is arguably Paul's most fascinating letter.

C. H. Talbert, *Reading Corinthians. A Literary and Theological Commentary on 1 and 2 Corinthians*. Crossroad, New York, 1987. Designed for Bible study groups, this book is rather too condensed for easy reading, but conveys a vast amount of background information.

NOTES

NOTES

NOTES

NOTES

NOTES

NOTES

NOTES

NOTES

NOTES